William E. Chandler

Letters of Mr. William E. Chandler relative to the so-called

southern policy of President Hayes

together with a letter to Mr. Chandler of Mr. William Lloyd Garrison

William E. Chandler

Letters of Mr. William E. Chandler relative to the so-called southern policy of President Hayes
together with a letter to Mr. Chandler of Mr. William Lloyd Garrison

ISBN/EAN: 9783337017859

Printed in Europe, USA, Canada, Australia, Japan

Cover: Foto ©ninafisch / pixelio.de

More available books at **www.hansebooks.com**

LETTERS

OF

MR. WILLIAM E. CHANDLER

RELATIVE TO THE SO-CALLED

Southern Policy of President Hayes,

TOGETHER WITH A LETTER TO MR. CHANDLER OF

MR. WILLIAM LLOYD GARRISON.

"I do not care for myself, but I do care for the poor colored men of the South. The colored man's fate will be worse than when he was in slavery."
"The loyal people of the South need special and powerful protection."
"Loyalty should be respected, and treason made odious."
"If you want a law faithfully and fairly administered, entrust power only to its friends."
                              RUTHERFORD B. HAYES.

"How he stands condemned out of his own mouth. How he has broken all his oft-repeated pledges of protection to those who, to save his election, heroically encountered terrible sufferings and deadly perils in getting to the polls."
                              WM. LLOYD GARRISON.

1878.
MONITOR AND STATESMAN OFFICE,
CONCORD, NEW HAMPSHIRE.
GIBSON BROTHERS, 1012 Penna. Ave., Washington, D. C.
[Where Orders should be addressed. See last page of cover.]

LETTERS

or

WM. E. CHANDLER.

[INTRODUCTORY NOTE.]

CONCORD, N. H., *February* 11, 1878.

Continued requests for copies of Mr. Chandler's letters have made necessary this edition, [in connection with which is published a letter from Mr. William Lloyd Garrison.]

Notwithstanding the criticisms and denunciations which the letters have elicited, none of the statements of fact therein have been effectively denied or disproved. No person named has made denial over his own signature, and various reported interviews have contained only evasions, or denials of facts not charged. The substantial correctness of all the facts stated in the letters is hereby re-affirmed.

Persistent attempts have been made by hostile newspapers to create the impression that the letters assail the title of President Hayes and propose to reopen the Presidential election-controversy. This misrepresentation was promoted by the fact that the telegraphic reports of the letters gave in full, point numbered IV, relative to the fulfilment of the Louisiana bargain, but only a brief summary of the remainder. An entire perusal of the letters will correct all misapprehension on this point. They contain expressions like the following:

" Unquestionably he should have asserted in every pos-
" sible way the moral and legal validity of his own title."

" Wisdom and honor, therefore, it seems to me, clearly
" required that President Hayes should maintain his own
" rightfulness of title. * * * Had he done so, in my

3

4

" belief, the Democratic cry of fraud would have been the
" merest folly."

In fact, instead of assailing the Presidential title, one
complaint in the letters is that President Hayes has himself
effected a taint upon his own title by his betrayal and destruction of the lawful governments of South Carolina and
Louisiana, and his abandonment of the principles of the
Republican party and adoption of the principles of the
Democratic party, which it is inconceivable that he would
have done if he had believed in his own rightfulness of title,
—and desired to stand by and vindicate it. Therefore, for
whatever re-agitation or re-investigation of the Presidential
question there may take place, the President and his advisers, the Louisiana bargainers who sold their republican
birthright for a mess of pottage, are responsible, and not
those Republicans who denounce and repudiate the trade
and the treason.

It may also be added that it cannot be possible that the
true interests of the Republican party are to be subserved
by denying or concealing any fact connected with the
Presidential canvass or countings. If any such exist dis-
creditable or dishonoring to the party or to the President,
to Secretary Sherman, or Senator Matthews, or Mr.
Chandler, or any other members of the party, the sooner
they are exposed, reprobated, and repudiated, the better
and safer for the future of Republican principles and the
Republican organization.

———

The briefest possible summary of the points of the letters is—

I. That President Hayes was chosen President by the
Republican party on a radical platform pledging federal
power to protect human rights and lawful governments at
the South; South Carolina and Louisiana giving him their
indispensable votes, and also electing Republican State
governments.

II. That after his actual installation, secured by a prior secret bargain that he should do so, he actively and personally tore down the lawful State governments of South Carolina and Louisiana, and established rebel mob governments in their stead; violated the Republican pledges to protect human rights and maintain the supremacy of the law, released negro-murderers whom he was elected to prosecute and punish, gave federal power at the South to rebel Democrats, glorified the rebel soldiers at the expense of Union soldiers, taunted the black race with its helplessness, and shamefully boasted of his betrayal of it.

III. That this, his degradation of himself and his betrayal of his party, has annihilated its organization at the South, making Republican ascendency there impossible, and has almost destroyed the party at the North, so that the only way to prevent a Democratic victory in 1880 by reason of a solid South and a divided North, is to promptly repudiate an administration and a policy which is dishonoring, paralyzing, and destroying the Republican party.

If to utter these facts and conclusions be treason, let the most be made of it. Mr. Chandler is content to rest upon the following endorsement by Mr. Garrison, whose unselfish devotion to the cause of human rights, and whose clear vision and calm judgment make his commendation, if not wholly deserved, yet most warmly gratifying:

" HONORING YOU FOR YOUR POLITICAL COURAGE AND PA-
" TRIOTIC FIDELITY, I AM EMULOUS TO MEET ANY AMOUNT OF
" PERSONAL DETRACTION IN COMMON WITH YOURSELF. ACTIVE
" AND SERVICEABLE AS YOU HAVE BEEN IN THE REPUBLICAN
" RANKS, YOU HAVE NEVER DONE, BECAUSE YOU COULD NOT
" HAVE DONE, AN ACT MORE HONORABLE TO THE REPUBLICAN
" PARTY, OR MORE IN ACCORDANCE WITH ITS REGISTERED PROM-
" ISES AND PLEDGES, OR MORE IMPORTANT TO PRESERVE ITS
" INTEGRITY TO THE CAUSE OF FREEDOM AND EQUAL RIGHTS,
" AND ITS SUPREMACY OVER THE LAND, THAN IN WRITING AND

6

" PUBLISHING YOUR LETTER TO THE REPUBLICANS OF NEW
" HAMPSHIRE. FEEL NO ANXIETY AS TO WHAT WILL BE THE
" JUDGMENT OF THE FUTURE, AND CARE NOTHING FOR THE
" DENUNCIATIONS OF THE MISLED AND TIME-SERVING.

" MY FAITH IN THE TRIUMPH OF THE RIGHT LIES IN THE NOT
" FAR DISTANT FUTURE, THOUGH FOR THE PRESENT IT IS BE-
" TRAYED.

" VERY TRULY YOURS,

" WM. LLOYD GARRISON.

" JANUARY 29, 1878."

To the Republicans of New Hampshire :

It is my privilege and duty as your representative on the Republican National Committee to state to you the reasons for my hostility to the so-called southern policy of the administration of President Hayes.

I.

The Presidential campaign of 1876 was carried on with no announced change of the principles of the Republican party concerning the Southern States lately in rebellion.

The Cincinnati Convention had declared the Republican party to be "sacredly pledged" to the complete protection of all the citizens of the South "in the free enjoyment of " all their rights." " We declare it to be the solemn obli- " gation of the Legislative and Executive Departments of " the Government to put in immediate exercise all their " constitutional powers * * * for securing to every " American citizen complete liberty and exact equality in " the exercise of all civil, political, and public rights. To " this end we imperatively demand a Congress and *Chief* " *Executive* whose COURAGE and FIDELITY to these duties " shall not falter until these results are placed beyond " dispute or recall."

Mr. George William Curtis, in the Convention, had commended his favorite candidate as one who, "armed " with the power of the Government of the United States " as district attorney of Kentucky, hunted and hunted and " hunted the Ku-Klux until the Ku-Klux disappeared." " The life of every man at the South is safe in the hands " of this man from Kentucky, who has known, as you of " the South have bitterly learned, * * * the mortal " perils of the struggle."

Governor Hayes, in his letter of acceptance, endorsed the resolutions, and specially declared himself in favor of " the complete protection of all citizens in the free enjoy- " ment of all their constitutional rights." "What the

" South needs most is peace, and peace depen 's upon the
" supremacy of the law. There can be no enduring peace
" if the constitutional rights of any portion ot the people
" are habitually disregarded."

The candidate for Vice-President, Hon. William A.
Wheeler, announced it to be the mission of the party to
secure " to every American citizen complete liberty and
" exact equality in the exercise of all civil, political, and
" public rights. This will be accomplished only when the
" American citizen, without regard to color, shall wear
" this panoply of citizenship as freely and securely in the
" canebrakes of Louisiana as on the banks of the St.
" Lawrence."

The Presidential campaign was carried on, so far as
methods and utterances were concerned, in no respects
differently from the campaigns of 1868 and 1872. The
duty of the Federal Government to interfere by all pos
sible constitutional and legal means for the protection of
life and a free ballot at the South, was the principal issue
of the contest. The " bloody shirt," as it is termed, was
freely waved, and Governor Hayes himself urged prominent public men to put forward, as our best argument, the
dangers of " rebel rule and a solid South."

On the 8th of November, when he thought himself defeated, he uttered these words : " I do not care for myself,
" * * * but I do care for the poor colored men of
" the South. * * * Northern men cannot live there,
" and will leave. * * * The Southern people will
" practically treat the constitutional amendments as nulli-
" ties, and then the colored man's fate will be worse than
" when he was in slavery. * * * That is the only
" reason I regret that the news is as it is."

On this main issue—the necessity of keeping Federal
power in Republican hands and using it for the protection
of black and white Southern Republicans—was the Presidential campaign, by Governor Hayes' advice and procurement, carried on and won.

II.

On the morning of the 8th of November it was apparent that Hayes and Wheeler were elected by One majority, if South Carolina, Florida, and Louisiana had given them their votes. But immediately the Tilden forces—hungry Northern and desperate Southern Democrats—determined to prevent the counting of the votes of those States for the Republican candidates; and threats, attempts to bribe, and all manner of foul influences were arrayed to seduce or intimidate the local Republican officials who were to declare the result.

To counteract these machinations, Governor Hayes sent a large array of distinguished persons to the contested States, from Ohio notably the following:

Messrs. John Sherman, (afterwards made Secretary of the
  Treasury;)
  Stanley Matthews, (private counsel for Governor
  Hayes; afterwards made U. S. Senator by his in-
  fluence;)
  Edward F. Noyes, (afterwards made Minister to
  France;)
  John Little, (Governor Hayes' Attorney-General;)
  Samuel Shellabarger, (Governor Hayes' private coun-
  sel;)
  James A. Garfield, (afterwards member of Electoral
  Commission and Administration candidate for
  Speaker,)
and many others went there from other sections.

In South Carolina and Florida, owing to the manifest facts and to the noble fearlessness of Governor Daniel H. Chamberlain and Governor Marcellus L. Stearns in protecting the canvassing boards, the correct result of the election—the choice of Hayes electors—was declared, without extraordinary assurances from the northern visitors.

In Louisiana, however, there had been thrown into the ballot-boxes over 7,000 more votes for the Tilden than for the Hayes electors, and to make Hayes President it became necessary for the Returning Board, acting under peculiar local laws, to throw out more than 7,000 Tilden votes on account of alleged murder, riot, and intimidation, preventing a fair and free election in certain parishes. To perform this extraordinary, even if justifiable, work in the face of an armed and infuriated Democracy required men of undaunted courage; and such courage the Returning Board possessed. It required also that the Board should have assurances that the national exigency demanded its performance; that the moral sentiment of the North would approve it; and that they themselves should be protected from evil consequences to be apprehended from the violence of a mob-government, which it was known would be established by one Nicholls, a pretender to the office of Governor against Stephen B. Packard who was sure to be found to be elected Governor if the Hayes electors should be found to have been chosen.

All these assurances were freely and forcibly given by Mr. Senator Sherman and his associates. Mr. Stanley Matthews declared to Mr. J. E. Leonard, and on more than one occasion, that Hayes and Packard should stand or fall together.

A reported interview of Governor Hayes, Dec. 3, with Mr. W. R. Roberts, of the New Orleans *Times*, having occasioned alarm as to the future course of the prospective President toward Southern Republicans and the Louisiana and South Carolina governments, Governor Hayes, through his private secretary, Captain A. E. Lee, (since made consul-general to Frankfort,) and General James M. Comly, of the Ohio State *Journal*, (since made Minister to the Sandwich Islands,) denied the reported interview, and all sympathy with the sentiments therein expressed.

Encouraged and forced forward by these assurances the Returning Board boldly performed its duty, gave voice to the murdered Republicans of the bull-dozed parishes of Louisiana, and made Hayes President and Packard Governor of Louisiana, by titles indissolubly connected in law, in morals, and by every rule of honor that prevails among civilized men.

The same tender regard for the Louisiana Republicans and for the result which they had achieved continued

during the ensuing struggle in Congress. The Returning
Board were arrested and confined at Washington by the
Confederate House of Representatives. Sick and in prison,
they were visited by Senator Sherman and his associates,
and urged to stand firm until relief should come from the,
advent to power of the President whom they had made.
Before the Electoral Commission, to maintain and vindicate
their work, Governor Hayes personally continued the em-
ployment of Messrs. Matthews and Shellabarger, while
Senator Sherman, from his place in the Senate, on Dec. 14,
threatened negro insurrections unless Hayes should be
counted in and the " poor colored men " placed under his
devoted care:

" There are other remedies, but I do not like to discuss
" them.   *   *   *

" We can teach the negroes that they have an inherent
" right of self-defence.   *   *   *   The negro might soon
" be taught, especially in those parishes where there are
" three black men to one white man, that he has the right
" of self-defence; but who wishes to even suggest, or inti-
" mate, or anticipate such horrors ? Who wishes to see a
" war of races ? Yet, rather than see what has occurred
" in Louisiana, these men will learn   *   *   *   that they
" can resent these outrages ; that the negro can defend his
" cabin, his wife, his children, from these outrages, and
" that he will be justified by the laws of God and man in
" repelling these assaults, whether they come by day or
" by night. I do not want to see this done ; I fear it, and
" yet it will come   *   *   *   unless you give to the ne-
" groes the rights which are secured to them by the Con-
" stitution of the United States.

" I do believe that under a wise policy, with an Admin-
" istration that will be firm in maintaining the rights of
" the blacks as well as be generous to the whites, all the
" clouds that are now lowering upon our house will pass
" away, and be in the deep bosom of the ocean buried."

With substantial unanimity the Republicans of the country seconded the determination of their representatives in
Congress to declare and achieve the election and inaugura-

tion of President Hayes; and the Republican party was never more courageous, harmonious, or united than on the day of his accession.

III.

Coming to the Presidency under these remarkable circumstances, what should have been President Hayes' course?

1. Unquestionably he should have asserted in every possible way the moral and legal validity of his own title, and of every step taken by his procurement or desire in the long series of events which established it.

2. He should have maintained faithful and scrupulous allegiance to the principles of the Republican party, by proclaiming which the victory had been won, and to the men of that party whose unprecedented efforts and courage had elevated him to a station of the highest honor and power as its representative.

3. Above all, he should have avoided any yielding or concession to the Democratic party, from which the Presidency had been so suddenly, unexpectedly, and exasperatingly wrested.

It is inconceivable that any wise or honorable man should be willing to take the Presidency, and then suffer or effect any taint upon his own title. Governor Hayes had it in his power at any moment, from November 8 to March 4, to avoid the responsibilities of the office, but thought not of doing it. On the contrary, at every stage in the progress of the countings, State and National, his active influence was present through his counsel, agents, and intimate friends, pressing forward the struggle. Not declining, but eagerly demanding and taking the place, it necessarily follows that he was bound to maintain the integrity of his claim thereto and of the means by which it was made effectual. Any other course would be sure to bring deserved condemnation and disgrace upon himself, the men of the party who had been prominent in his behalf, and upon the party itself.

To make concessions to the defeated Democracy and to abandon the principles of his own party would not only proclaim his doubts as to the rightfulness of his own election, but would also be an admission that such election, even if rightful and honest, was undesirable for the country.

If the men and principles of the Democratic party were to control the country, why should they not do so through Samuel J. Tilden, their appropriate representative? Why the protracted labor, the high excitement, the dangerous struggle, the death or ruin of Southern Republicans, if the principles of the Republican party were to be abandoned and the Administration to be made Democratic in all respects except in name?

Wisdom and honor, therefore, it seems to me, clearly required that President Hayes should maintain his own rightfulness of title, and stand by the men and principles of his party. Had he done so, in my belief, the Democratic cry of fraud would have been the merest folly; the Republican party would have remained dominant in every Northern State and in several Southern States, and would have swept the country in the recent fall elections. Instead of all this what do we see?

IV.

Almost the first act of the new Administration was to fulfil a bargain that had been made during the Presidential count, by which, if Hayes should be President, the lawful governments of Louisiana and South Carolina were to be abandoned, and the mob-governments in those States were to be recognized and established.

Certain Democrats in the House of Representatives, seeing that, by the recurring decisions of the Electoral Commission and the regular proceedings of the two Houses under the electoral bill which they had warmly supported, Hayes would surely be President, had conceived the plan of saving something from the wreck. They had, therefore, threatened by dilatory motions and riotous proceedings to break up the count, and then opened negotiations with such timid or too eagerly expectant Republicans as they could find ready. They had succeeded beyond their most sanguine expectations. Senator Sherman had visited Ohio and consulted Governor Hayes. Mr. Henry Watterson, a Democratic member, and a nephew of Mr. Stanley Matthews, had acted as go-between; and on the one side Messrs. Matthews, Charles Foster, John Sherman, James A. Garfield, and on the other, L. Q. C. Lamar, John B. Gordon, E. J. Ellis, Randall Gibson, E. A. Burke, and John Young Brown, had agreed (1) that the count should not be broken up in the House, but that Hayes should be declared and inaugurated President, and (2) that upon Hayes' accession the troops should be withdrawn from protecting Governors Chamberlain and Packard, and that the new Administration should recognize the governments of Wade Hampton, in South Carolina, and F. H. Nicholls, in Louisiana.

By certain general and indefinite letters since given to the public, by a secret writing now in the hands of E. A. Burke, and in other ways, the agreement was authenticated; and President Grant was immediately requested by Governor Hayes' counsel on no account to recognize Packard or Chamberlain, but to leave the ultimate decision as to their fate to the incoming President.

After the inauguration the bargain was speedily fulfilled. As soon as the electoral vote of their States was safe, Governors Packard and Chamberlain had been notified by Messrs. Matthews and Evarts to get out. Governor Chamberlain was now summoned to Washington and informed that he must surrender. He protested against his taking-off. The President hesitated, but Wade Hampton demanded the performance of the bargain. Mr. Matthews was sent for, came from Ohio, and within twenty-four hours the United States flag was ordered down in Charleston and Governor Chamberlain stamped out.

As to Louisiana, the fulfillment proceeded more slowly, but none the less surely. Packard had made, March 21st, a constitutional call for Federal aid, which it was difficult to withhold from one as surely Governor as Hayes was President. And yet there was the bargain.

As a subterfuge, an unconstitutional commission, consisting of

Messrs. John M. Harlan,
Joseph R. Hawley,
C. B. Lawrence,
Wayne McVeagh,
John C. Brown,

was sent to New Orleans, instructed gradually to destroy the Packard Legislature by seducing or forcing its members into the Nicholls Legislature. But they proving too stubbornly Republican, the commission telegraphed the President that nothing would destroy Packard but the actual order withdrawing the troops. At the word, the President gave the order, Packard was crushed, and the commission returned triumphant to Washington, to be "recognized"— one of them, General Harlan, by an appointment as Supreme Court Judge; another, Mr. Lawrence, by the release of Jake Rehm, the great whiskey conspirator and defrauder of the revenue at Chicago; General Hawley was offered the appointment as Chief Commissioner to the Paris Exhibition, but declined because the salary was to be only five thousand dollars; and three offices were tendered to Mr. McVeagh, but declined on the ground that his signal services demanded more ample recognition; the English mission was next assigned him, but circumstances have made its delivery inexpedient or impossible.

One other hope remained to Governor Packard. He had a lawful court of justice, and might appeal to that. But there were two vacancies, and it required all three of the judges, Ludeling, Leonard, and John E. King, to make a quorum. Judge King was immediately appointed collector of New Orleans, Packard's court was struck down and the Nicholls mob-government reigned supreme. The bargain was in every way fulfilled, and Mr. Burke had no occasion, as had been threatened, to make public the secret agreement. Hayes had been made President by the fidelity and courage of Packard and Chamberlain and their devoted followers, and his Administration had trampled them down.

V.

In further pursuance of the bargain made with the Southern Democrats, the new Administration has adopted a so-called Southern policy, (1,) entirely contrary to the announced principles of the Republican party, (2,) which has been carried out by the abandonment of all Federal intention and effort to protect life, property, or suffrage at the South, or to enforce the constitutional amendments, and (3) has resulted in the enforced dissolution of the Republican party at the South, and its demoralization, division, and defeats at the North.

Senator Dawes at Faneuil Hall, November 2, in defending what he admits to be a change—a new departure—bases it upon the proposition that "when the rebels laid "down their arms, the States and the people fell back at "once into their old position, every one of them with as "much power as before the war. The rebel went from "the battle-field to the ballot-box, and stood there equal "with his conqueror."

Messrs. Charles Foster and Stanley Matthews, in their written guarantee of February 26, 1877, to John B. Gordon and John Young Brown, define the new policy to be to give the Southern States "the right to control their own "affairs in their own way"; and John Young Brown so describes it in his account of the bargain.

By the *New York Tribune* of September 26, it appears that "Governor Wade Hampton is still with the party, "and is introduced by the President to every audience as "an honest and patriotic man," and that at Atlanta, Hampton said of the President: "When I saw him carrying out "the policy for twelve years advocated by the Democratic "party, I said I would sustain him in that policy as long "as he continued in that path."

President Hayes himself also calls his new policy only

the application of the principle of " local self-government," ✗
and thus eulogizes the Georgians who are to be entrusted
with it :

" You, here, mainly joined the Confederate side and
" fought bravely ; risked your lives heroically in behalf of
" your convictions. And can any true man, anywhere, fail
" to respect the man who risks his life for his convictions ?"

At Chattanooga, September 20, he said : "As I demand
" respect from the man I found fighting against me for my
" convictions, I yield the same measure of respect to him
" who fought for his convictions."

At Gallatin, Tennessee, he said : " We have differed in
" the past, but we have fought out that difference. Those
" among you who fought and risked your lives did so for
" your principles. We fought and risked our lives on the
" opposite side for our convictions, and men who can do
" that can meet and look each other in the face with respect
" always."

At Atlanta, September 23, he said : " So, with no dis-
" credit to you and no special credit to us, the war turned
" out as it did."

Having thus blotted out all distinctions between loyalty ┼
and treason, between Union and rebel soldiers, between the
torturers of Andersonville and the veterans of the North,
he is equally explicit as to what he means to do for the
poor colored men, whom he pitied so much November 8 :
" And, now, my colored friends, listen.   *   *   *   After
" thinking it over, I believed that your rights and interests
" would be safer if the great mass of intelligent white men
" were LET ALONE by the General Government."

His confidence in his new friends is complete.   At Chattanooga also he tells the colored people : " Our confidence
" is perfect, that with the bayonets removed from the South
" the people of the South would be safer in every right, in
" every interest, than they ever were when protected merely
" by the bayonet."

As the policy of the Democratic party was to be carried
out at the South, a Southern Confederate general, Mr. D.
M. Key, a Democrat, who had opposed Hayes' election, and,

18

in the Senate, denounced his title as fraudulent, was appointed Postmaster-General, and commenced the distribution of the Southern post offices to rebel Democrats.

The negro-murderers of Hamburg and Ellenton had been indicted in the Federal courts of South Carolina. The great and good Hampton appealed for their release, and it was accorded by the President, in a letter of May 12, granting general amnesty to negro-murderers as "political offenders." To make immunity more certain, the policy of appointing as district attorneys and marshals men agreeable to the white people of the South—that is, Democrats, —was determined upon.

At the dictation of the most trusted and potent adviser of the Administration, General Gordon—captured by Grant in 1865, put in Federal command by Hayes in 1876—one O. P. Fitzsimmons, a rebel Democrat and a cousin of Wade Hampton, was appointed marshal of Georgia, in place of one Smythe, a competent and honest Republican, and was confirmed by the Democratic Senators' votes and that of Stanley Matthews alone.

Prior to the selection of Fitzsimmons, the President had determined to change Smythe and appoint Mr. W. A. Huff, of Macon, a Democrat whom Gordon had selected. Some Republicans of Georgia joined in recommending Huff; upon discovering which damning fact Gordon retracted his selection of Huff and procured the President to nominate Fitzsimmons.

Gordon thus states his reasons in a letter to Huff:

"I heard for the first time that you were being pressed for appointment as a suitable person to build up the Republican party in Georgia. Surprised at this, I at once asked the President to withhold any appointment for a day, and until I could be heard from. The President consented."

"Messrs. McBurney and Dibble, Republicans from Macon, * * * say in their letter to the President that your appointment would materially strengthen Republicanism in Georgia, in harmonizing conflicting party differences, and bring much strength from sources hitherto dormant, or in active opposition."

" I therefore asked the President the direct question : ' Is Mr. Huff urged for appointment as a Democrat ?' He said No : not as a Democrat, but as a man with very liberal ideas in politics."

" The information given me by the President himself, supplemented by the fact that Messrs. McBurney and Dibble had presented and urged your appointment because it would materially strengthen Republicanism in Georgia were the reasons, the only reasons, and I think sufficient reasons, for my opposition to your appointment."

" They left me no alternative but to say to the President that I did not believe your appointment would be acceptable to the people of Georgia."

" Had you made known your disapproval of such arguments, you would have saved the President from any misapprehension as to your political status, me from the disagreeable task which a sense of duty to my State compelled me to perform, and yourself, possibly, from the mortification experienced at the loss of the office you desire to fill.

J. B. GORDON."

And so General Gordon procures Samuel J. Tilden—no, Rutherford B. Hayes !—to turn out Smythe, a Republican, change from Huff, a liberal Democrat, to Fitzsimmons, a rebel Democrat, and make the latter marshal to protect the poor colored people of Georgia !

Of a like character, procured by like influences, are the appointments of Waldron as marshal of Tennessee, and Northrop and his assistant as district attorneys in South Carolina.

These significant instances of a surrender of the power of the Federal courts to rebel Democrats, the prompt and complete amnesty to all negro-murderers and Ku-Klux, and the eager trampling out of the only remaining Republican State governments at the South, entirely crushed all Republican courage, and left Republicans at the mercy of their enraged enemies, who turned upon them with fierce hatred.

Persecutions and prosecutions in the State courts have been freely resorted to, and obnoxious Republicans driven away or unjustly convicted. The Republican party has been compelled to disband, and the dangers of a solid South and rebel rule, which President Hayes wanted the people of Ohio made to believe would be averted if he were elected, have become terrible realities.

In Mississippi, Governor Stone, infamous for his failure to prosecute effectually the Chisholm murderers, was re-elected by 96,382 votes, only 1,168 Republicans daring to go to the polls, where, in 1872, Grant had 82,175 votes and Greeley only 47,288, and in 1876 Hayes had 52,605 votes to 112,173 for Tilden.

In Virginia, 101,940 Democratic votes were cast and 4,389 Republican.

In Georgia, the Republican party, seeing Senators Gordon and Hill the intimate friends and trusted advisers of President Hayes, dictating the appointments and controlling the Federal patronage, must of necessity dissolve, and yet, in 1872, Grant had 62,550 votes and Greeley 76,356, and even Hayes had 50,446 to 130,068 for Tilden.

In Pennsylvania, where Hayes had 384,122 votes to 366,158 for Tilden, the Republican party, in 1877, weighted by the Hayes policy, cast but 244,480 votes, a falling off of 140,000, and the Democrats carried the State by 7,000 majority.

In Ohio, where Hayes had 330,698 to 323,182 for Tilden, the Republican party, in 1877, cast only 241,437 votes, a loss of 89,261, and lost the State by 27,000 majority and the legislature by over 40 majority, which the previous year had been Republican by 35 majority.

In Massachusetts, where the new policy was most offensively thrust down the throats of Republicans, of the 150,063 voters for Hayes, who gave him 42,000 majority over Tilden, over 70,000 refused to vote for Governor Rice in 1877, and the majority against him was 1,836, and it was only by the support and money of the organized rumsellers of the State, and over 10,000 Democratic votes procured by rum influence, that he secured his election by a plurality, and the State was saved from the fate of Ohio and Pennsylvania.

Look, however, at the result where the new policy was repudiated.

In Iowa, Hayes had 59,228 plurality, and in 1877 the Republicans had 51,823 plurality.

In New York, Tilden had 32,742 majority, and in 1877 the Democrats had only 11,264 majority, although the new-policy men promoted the Democratic side by indifference and by procuring the new Administration to make or announce many injudicious removals of Federal officers for the sole purpose of irritating and humiliating Senator Conkling and his friends.

VI.

These, then, are the facts before us :

I. Rutherford B. Hayes was elected President by the Republican party on the platform of opposition to rebel rule and a solid South, and with pledges to protect, to the extent of Federal power, life, suffrage, and the free exercise of all political rights at the South; was counted in as President only by reason of special pledges to the same effect given by his representatives and agents, Senator Sherman and other Ohio emissaries, who particularly and emphatically promised that he would recognize and maintain the lawful State governments of South Carolina and Louisiana, and stand by Governors Chamberlain and Packard.

II. Before the actual declaration of his election, and to secure the same, a deliberate written bargain was made in his behalf by the same Senator Sherman and his associates, by which it was agreed with Senator Gordon and other Southern rebel Democrats that when he should be President no attempt should be made to enforce the above principles of his party, but that the South should be allowed to manage its own affairs in its own way, and that, in particular, he would abandon the lawful State governments of Louisiana and South Carolina, and recognize in their stead the mob-governments of Wade Hampton and F. H. Nicholls.

III. After his inauguration, the bargain was literally fulfilled; the United States flag disgracefully hauled down in Columbia and New Orleans; the lawful governments notified to surrender to rebel mobs, and, upon their hesitation, deliberately and actively torn down by his Administration by unconstitutional processes and the use of Federal patronage, vigorously wielded by the same Secretary Sherman and his associates; the mob governments of Hampton and Nicholls recognized, and a solid South and rebel-rule established by the swift and eager action of his Administration.

IV. All attempts to administer the Government upon the principles by proclaiming which he had been elected and counted in, were deliberately abandoned; the South notified that it should not be interfered with by his Administration; Southern Ku-Klux and negro-murderers released and amnestied by Presidential order; the enforcement of Federal laws at the South given up, or intrusted to rebel Democratic hands: Senator Gordon and his fellow-bargainers accepted as the intimate and acknowledged advisers of the President and the disposers of Federal patronage; and the black and white Republicans of the South mercilessly surrendered to the insults, persecutions, and atrocities of their Democratic enemies.

V. As a necessary result of all this, the Republican party at the South was disbanded and no Republican votes were cast in States where a free ballot would show large Republican majorities; the Republican party at the North was paralyzed wherever the advice of supporters or apologists for the new policy was heeded; Republican defeats ensued wherever it was endorsed, Republican victories only where it was repudiated: and with a solid South and a divided North, the confederate Democrats are marching towards a national victory in 1880, while President Hayes and Secretary Sherman look on with as much indifference as if they were in name, as they are in fact, allies of the Democratic party.

VII.

In view of these lamentable facts, it is the duty of true Republicans to take prompt and courageous action.

Silence is a crime; acquiescence and inaction are political death. Can the Republican party, of heroic achievements, be bound to an Administration which is not a free agent, but is bound by a bargain to Generals Gordon, L. Q. C. Lamar, Wade Hampton, and other Southern Democrats now in high office only through the blood of murdered Republicans? Does not every voter in the land know that Hayes and Packard were elected simultaneously, and held by the same title, and that when Hayes abandoned and trampled down Packard he put an irremovable stain upon his own title? The Republican party has lived long, and survived many assaults and many treasons, only because it has been a party founded upon high principles, animated by lofty sentiment, courageously acting up to noble convictions. If it now disgraces its record, and endorses or fails to repudiate the Hayes surrender, its voters will leave it by thousands; its days are numbered; it will die a deserved and an unhonored death.

But such is not to be its fate, at least not with the consent of the Republicans of New Hampshire. In twenty-seven elections since 1855, they have successfully battled for Radical Republican principles. They sent out the soldiers of the State to fight Generals Gordon and Lamar on the battle-field. When, three years ago, these same Confederate Generals came to teach the men of the Granite State their political duties, they were followed back to Washington by news of a Republican majority largely increased by their harangues. They will receive a similar greeting in March, 1878, but it will not result from endorsing a Presidential policy which has surrendered to them the Federal patronage of Georgia and Mississippi, and has forgiven the murders of hundreds of their fellow-citizens, committed that they might rise to political power, bargain with the agents of a Republican President, and dominate in the White House; and when that policy has been repudiated by the Republican party of the nation; when the North has been again aroused to the dangers of a solid South and rebel rule, which it vainly attempted to avert by the election of Rutherford B. Hayes; when it shall have again resumed the work planned, but not accomplished, by the Cincinnati Convention of 1876, of " secur- " ing to every American citizen complete liberty and exact " equality in the exercise of all civil, political and public " rights," by means of a " Chief Executive whose COURAGE " AND FIDELITY shall not falter till these results are placed " beyond dispute or recall "—(so that William Lloyd Garrison and Wendell Phillips can canvass Georgia and Mississippi, and colored citizens vote there, as freely as Gordon and Lamar can canvass New Hampshire and Democrats vote there)—then, and then only, will there be " national pacification " and " enduring peace," and the mission of the Republican party will be completed.

W. E. CHANDLER.

CONCORD, N. H., Dec. 26, 1877.

Editor Monitor:

Will you allow me to prove by the *New York Tribune* files alone—

I. That while Hayes was being counted in President, by the vote of Louisiana, a bargain was made that the lawful government of that State should be surrendered to the Nicholls mob-government.

II. That such bargain was fulfilled by the new Administration, which deliberately and actively destroyed a lawful State government calling upon it for protection against a mob, and established a pretended State government set up by that mob.

III. That the principal agency in fulfilling such bargain was an unconstitutional commission, instructed to destroy, and which did destroy, the legal and set up the mob government; which commission has been, and is to be, rewarded by Federal offices for their misdeeds.

If the following extracts, taken literally (except the appropriate headings) from the *Tribune*, do not satisfactorily prove the above propositions, then call for the original bargain now in possession of E. A. Burke, and held as a weapon over the Republicans who made it.

Very respectfully,
WM. E. CHANDLER.

The Bargain.

LAMAR AND ELLIS BEGAN IT.

Tribune, March 30, 1877, p. 5.

[L. Q. C. Lamar to Ellis, Feb. 20, 1877, relative to Charles Foster's speech :]

" Foster said to a gentleman   *   *   *   that he made it after consultation with Mr. Matthews, Mr. Hayes' brother-in-law, and that Mr. Matthews urged him to say squarely that Hayes would have nothing to do with or say to Packard;   *   *   *   and further said, 'If I were to speak, I should say it, because it is the truth.'

" I think you should at once see Mr. Stanley Matthews, and ask him if President Hayes will give you some assurance that Hayes will not maintain Packard in his domination of your people.

"L. Q. C. LAMAR."

John Young Brown followed it up.

Tribune, March 29, 1877, p. 1.

[John Young Brown interview in *Courier-Journal* as to conference of Feb. 26.]

" I had come to request of him [Chas. Foster] written assurances that if Gov. Hayes was inaugurated he would restore home-rule in the States of Louisiana and South Carolina, and that the people of these States should control their affairs in their own way, as free from any intervention by the Federal authority as the State of Ohio."

" He agreed to give me the desired letter, and said he would also request Stanley Matthews to sign it.

" He came about midnight, and said he had that evening procured a meeting of some gentlemen from Louisiana and South Carolina, at Wormley's Hotel, at which also the Hon. Henry Watterson was present."

" Next day he gave the letters." * * * * " told me that President Grant would, as soon as the count was completed, issue a certain order to Gen. Augur, in Louisiana. * * The order was issued by Gen. Grant. The Hon. Charles Foster secured the inauguration of the President. Except for these letters, the result would never have been reached."

———

Senator Sherman saw Governor Hayes about it and other matters.

Tribune, Feb. 24, 1877, p. 7.

"COLUMBUS, O., *Feb.* 23.

" Senator Sherman will be chosen as Secretary of the Treasury. * * * Senator Sherman returned to Washington this afternoon."

———

A Cover was made for the Real Bargain.

Tribune, March 29, 1877, p. 1.

[Charles Foster's letter to J. Young Brown and John B. Gordon, Feb. 26, 1877.]

" Gov. Hayes' policy as to the status of certain Southern States * * * to have adopted such a policy as will give to the people of the States of South Carolina and Louisiana the right to control their own affairs in their own way, * * * authorized * * * to pledge ourselves to you for him that such will be his policy.

"CHAS. FOSTER."

[Matthews and Foster to same, Feb. 27—same except as follows:]

" We have the most emphatic confidence that such will be the policy of his administration.

"STANLEY MATTHEWS.
"CHAS. FOSTER."

E. A. Burke has a Secret Writing Covering it.

Tribune, April 2, 1877, p. 1.

WASHINGTON, *April* 1.

[Telegram from New Orleans reports interview with Major E. A. Burke as to the first agreement touching Louisiana affairs, consummated at Wormley's Hotel, where he appeared "as the representative of the Nicholls government."]

"He has a copy of that paper, but does not feel at liberty to make its contents known. The original parties thereto are bound not to divulge their knowledge of its purport, except in the event of a violation of faith on the part of those making the pledge."

"The provisions of the yet secret agreement, to which Secretary Sherman is a party, Major Burke says are dignified."

"Mr. Ellis and John Young Brown, he believes, supposed that the agreement referred to stipulated that the troops should be withdrawn from the vicinity of the Louisiana State-house on Wednesday last, and that failure to procure the necessary order by that time convinced them that they were released from any further secrecy. On the other hand, Major Burke asserts that there has not been the slightest intimation of a violation of the pledges. He expected that they would have been carried out before this time; but he asserts that as yet nobody has proved false to the pledges."

———

Foster admits an agreement, but denies a bargain.

Tribune, March 29, 1877, p. 1.

[Interview with Foster; he admits informal meeting; present as friends of Hayes, Sherman, Garfield, Dennison, Matthews; admits withdrawal of troops talked of and giving of letters, but says no bargains made.]

———

President Grant asked by Hayes to commence fulfilling it.

Tribune, March 1, 1877, p. 1.

WASHINGTON, *Feb.* 28.

"The President (Grant) has determined, * * * as soon as Governor Hayes is officially declared to be President-elect, to modify the orders to Gen. Augur; * * *

the result * * * would undoubtedly be the immediate surrender of Governor Packard and the universal recognition of Governor Nicholls. This policy * * * is understood to have the approval of Gov. Hayes' most intimate friends in this city, and probably * * * of Gov. Hayes himself. The Democrats are very much encouraged by the announcement of this new policy towards Louisiana, and will probably show their appreciation of it to-morrow by a more determined stand against the fillibusters than they have yet made at any time."

"It is reported that the Louisiana Conservatives have agreed to elect (as Senators) any two men whom a committee of Northern Republicans may name. As members of this committee, the names of Charles Foster, Stanley Matthews, * * * and others are mentioned. They are to select * * * one Republican and one moderate Conservative."

Fulfillment of Bargain— Tribune characterizes it.

Tribune, March 8, 1877, p. 1.

[Discusses Administration way out of difficulty.]

WASHINGTON, *March* 7.

"Influences might be brought to bear to induce a portion of the Packard legislature to go over to Nicholls, so as to give his legislature an unquestioned quorum. Then, in the exercise of its undoubted power, the legislature could undo the work of the Packard body, and confirm Nicholls in his claims. This plan savors of bargaining too much to be relished by high-minded men."

John M. Harlan, C. B. Lawrence, Joseph R. Hawley, and Wayne Mc Veagh employed to fulfil it.

Tribune, April 4, 1877.

[Secretary Evarts to Harlan-Louisiana-Commission, April 2, 1877.]

" The service desired of and entrusted to this commission does not involve any examination into, or report upon, the facts of the recent State election. * * * Devote your first and principal attention to a removal of the obstacles to an acknowledgment of one government. * * * If these obstacles should prove insuperable from whatever reason, and the hope of a single government in all its departments be disappointed, it should be your next endeavor to accomplish the recognition of a single legislature as the depository of the representative will of the people of Louisiana. * * * Your report of the result of this endeavor will satisfy the President of the wisdom of his selection."

Packard thinks the law and not bargains should be fulfilled.

Tribune, April 6, 1877, p. 1.

[Packard to President, April 5, requesting Commission to be instructed to inquire]

" 1. Which is the legal government entitled to recognition ?

"2. Which is the legal judiciary ?

" 3. Do domestic violence and insurrection prevail ? "

The Commission begin to strike at Packard.

Tribune, April 7, p. 1.

NEW ORLEANS, *April* 6.

" The commission began work to-day with great industry." * * * " The commissioners appear hopeful of bringing about a settlement."

The Commission begin Seduction of Packard's Legislature. Mr. Mc Veagh works in private.

Tribune, April 12, p. 5.

NEW ORLEANS, *April* 11.

"The commission are hopeful of reaching a result in a day or two satisfactory to themselves and the country. Their purpose still is to get a legislature together which they can say to the President represents beyond question the people of Louisiana. This they think will be accomplished * * * by the further desertion of members from the Packard to the Nicholls legislature. * * * One more colored member went over to-day. Only five more are needed. That number would have abandoned Gov. Packard to-day if the plan had not been revealed last night." * * * "The commission has been busy as

usual to-day." * * * "Besides this, the commissioners have been busy as individuals, but they do not state
what progress has been made."

Commission tell the President Republicans are Stalwart.

Tribune, April 13, 1877, p. 1.

WASHINGTON, *April* 12.

"The commission's session, which lasted until five this
morning, was considering the message to the President."
* * * "The Louisiana Commissioners to-day sent to
the President a long dispatch in cypher."

Mr. Evarts hurries them up in cypher.

Tribune, April 14, p. 1.

WASHINGTON, April 13.—"The commission are wrestling
to-night with a rather enigmatical cypher dispatch from Mr.
Evarts in reply to their request for further instructions."
"Yesterday the commission hoped to finish their work in
time to leave to-morrow night."

E. V. S. helps strike Packard.

Tribune April 14, p. 2.

E. V. S. says, April 7,—"Just now, the commissioners,
faithful to their instructions in Secretary Evarts' letter, are
laboring to secure a compromise legislature."

---

*One or two Commissioners conscientious—Mr. McVeagh says
he can wipe out Packard if troops are withdrawn.*

Tribune, April 16, p. 1.

NEW ORLEANS, April 15.—"The Louisiana controversy
is practically settled. The delay is occasioned by a difficulty in harmonizing all the members of the commission."
"This project for settlement is so completely a triumph for
the Nicholls party that it scarcely breaks the fall of Gov.
Packard. It is not expected that he will accept it with

good grace, if at all; but the commission are assured that as soon as it is promulgated a break will occur in the Packard legislature so large as to leave him no shadow of hope to maintain himself. The commission will recommend the withdrawal of the troops from the State-house, and the last vestige of the Packard government will disappear without violence or excitement."

———

Tribune, April 17, p. 1.

NEW ORLEANS, April 16.—The commission "cannot agree, it is believed, to recommend the withdrawal of the troops as a last resort to effect a settlement, two members being fearful of going on record as advising the President to throw overboard the Republican party of Louisiana." "The radicalism of these two commissioners appears to have delayed bringing matters to a point for nearly a week."

———

Packard begs the President to relieve him of his enemies, the Commissioners.

Tribune, April 17, p. 1.

Governor Packard to President, April 16:

"The reported purpose of the Administration, to carry out the suggestions of Messrs. Foster and Matthews by the withdrawal of the United States troops, is a steady menace to the Republicans in this State."

"The commission thus far has only suggested methods which directly tend to an abandonment of the contest, irrespective of right or justice."

———

Commission working hard—confident of wiping out Packard's Legislature if President will withdraw troops.

Tribune, April 18, p. 5.

NEW ORLEANS, April 17.—"The members of the commission, who are actively working to effect an adjustment, are confident that the end will be reached in a day or two. When the Republican leaders, who control a dozen or so of negro votes apiece, in the Packard legislature, and want to trade on them, can get no better terms than now offered, they will take their followers over to the Nicholls camp."

Tribune, April 19, p. 5.

NEW ORLEANS, *April* 18.—"The members of the commission predict, however, that there will be only one legislature in existence 48 hours from to-night. It is expected that this consummation will be brought about by a desertion of a portion of Gov. Packard's legislature while the commission are here, or by a general break-up following their departure."

"The departure of the commission, followed by an order fixing a time a few days in advance for the withdrawal of the troops from the vicinity of the State-House, will unquestionably dissipate the Packard government without collision or even excitement."

Packard's dissolution approaches — Commission in good spirits.

Tribune, April 20, p. 1.

NEW ORLEANS, *April* 19, Thursday.

"The commission have completed the work they came to do. To-day they informed the President of the existence of a legislature with an undisputed quorum." "The Packard legislature now becomes a rump without legal status, and its disintegration will proceed with accelerating rapidity." "The commission are well satisfied with the situation." "The commissioners talked freely, believing that the end of their labors is near. * * * They say they have strenuously endeavored to secure one legislature." "The commissioners are in good spirits over the present aspect of affairs."

Commission say cannot break up Packard's heroes until you actually withdraw troops—President withdraws them instanter.

Tribune, April 21, p. 1.

WASHINGTON, *April* 20.

"The President signed an order at 4.30 P. M. to-day, directing the U. S. troops quartered in New Orleans to be drawn from their present positions at noon on Tuesday next." "The effect of the act of the Executive to-day was apparently seen in New Orleans within an hour after it occurred. Before six o'clock a dispatch was received from ex-Governor Warmoth, announcing that the fight was over, and that he and his friends had stampeded to the Nicholls legislature, and that Gov. Packard had no longer a quorum in either house of his legislature." "It is believed that the other supporters of Gov. Packard will now desert, and that Packard, like Chamberlain, will give up the contest."

"The adjustment, though not arrived at in exactly the same way as was suggested by Mr. Evarts in his communication to the commission, is scarcely less satisfactory to the Administration." "It is now believed that by the middle of next week the Louisiana question will have become as much a matter of history as the late controversy in South Carolina, and that it will no longer require the attention of the Administration, which will then be able to devote its time to other contemplated reforms," (*sic*.)

Commission stay to sit on the Corpse.

Tribune, April 21, p. 1.

NEW ORLEANS, *Apr.* 20—*Friday.*

"The commission have decided to remain until to-morrow evening * * * in order to watch the further disintegration of the Packard government." "Five more members deserted Gov. Packard to-day."

The Tribune gives the dying Packard a blow.

Tribune, April 21, p. 1.

First editorial: "Freedom will shriek as Packard tumbles at noon of Tuesday next."

Packard still dying—President's order killed him with " neatness and dispatch"—Commissioners happy—Negro-killers offer them a banquet.

Tribune, April 23, p. 1.

NEW ORLEANS, *April* 22.

" Nothing is left of the Packard government except Gov. Packard himself and his metropolitan police guard. *The President's order for the withdrawal of the troops broke up the legislature with neatness and dispatch.*"

" The commission seemed to be highly gratified at the
absence of resentment on the part of the Nicholls party."
" The commission closed their labors to-day, and left for
Washington." " The commission have devoted themselves
in the most laborious manner to their work." " It was understood that a public reception was tendered them by the
people of this city, but declined with thanks." " It is
known here that the Louisiana commission telegraphed the
President Friday morning, advising an immediate announcement of the withdrawal of the troops."

No more life in Packard, unless he gets into the Courts.

Tribune, April 25, p. 1.

NEW ORLEANS, *April* 20.

" Now that the commission has closed its labors, the
work it has done can, for the first time, be correctly judged."
" It has accomplished the task set for it to do."

WASHINGTON, *April* 24.

" All the members of the commission express themselves as entirely satisfied with the result of their labors."

" The commission do not expect that he (Packard) will
cause any public disturbance, but they are not so certain
that he will not refer the question of his title to the courts."

*Commission claim that they killed Packard by their timely
demand for withdrawal of Troops.*

Tribune, April 26, p. 2.

Report of John M. Harlan-Commission, April 25:
" It is proper that we should say * * * that we were
induced to suggest in our telegram of the 20th instant that
the immediate announcement of the time when the troops
would be withdrawn to their barracks would be better for
the peace of Louisiana than to postpone the announcement
to some distant day."

Packard tells the People how it was done.

Tribune, April 26, p. 2.

Gov. Packard to people of Louisiana, April 25:

"The commission found the legal legislature still in session at the State-House." * * * "The result of their labors during the two weeks they remained here is known of all men." * * * "They induced a number of members of the legal house of representatives to take seats in the Nicholls house, thus giving it a returning-board quorum." * * * "This result having been achieved, it is a matter of record that congratulatory messages were exchanged between the President and his commission. On the following day the President by a formal order, made public through the press, directed that the United States troops occupying a building in the vicinity of the State-House should be removed to their barracks."

Packard's Court destroyed by appointing Judge John E. King Collector—Judge Leonard reserved for future seduction— Packard now buried.

Tribune, April 30.

WASHINGTON, *April* 29.

"The President has decided to appoint Judge J. E. King to the collectorship of New Orleans." "This appointment is one of great importance and practically removes one of the few remaining obstacles to the success of the President's policy in Louisiana. Judge King is one of the justices of the Packard supreme court. The Packard supreme court has always been considered by the President as in law one of the strongest departments of the Packard government." "The best lawyers her e, including Secretary Evarts, are of the opinion that the legality and constitutionality of the Packard supreme court was almost beyond controversy."

"The appointment of Judge King seems to solve this difficulty. The Packard court, under the constitution, should be composed of five members, and only three were ever appointed by Governor Kellogg—Judges King, Leonard, and Ludeling. These three constituted a quorum. Without a quorum the court cannot exist, and without the attendance of each one of these three a quorum is impossible. As to the two remaining judges who should technically make up the court, they can never be appointed, because even if Governor Packard should nominate two persons, he would have no senate to confirm them. The abandonment of the court, therefore, by any one of these three members works its effectual dissolution. Judge King will accept the office of collector, and Judge Leonard is already elected to Congress from a district in which there is no contest, and will of course be seated."

The Commissioners return in triumph—"Well done, good and faithful servants. Enter thou into the joy of thy Lord."

GENERAL HARLAN RECOGNIZED.

Tribune, Dec. 11.

"WASHINGTON, *Dec.* 10.

"Between 11 and 12 * * * the Chief Justice said he had received the commission of John M. Harlan as an Associate Justice. * * * The oath will now be taken.

* * * 'I, John M. Harlan, do solemnly swear that I will *administer justice* without respect to persons, and *do equal right to the poor and to the rich.*

'JOHN M. HARLAN.'"

C. B. Lawrence gets Jake Rehm, Chicago whiskey-thief, released.

Tribune, May 4.

"WASHINGTON, *May* 3.

"Attorney-General Devens telegraphed to-day to District-Attorney Bangs to postpone the Rehm case for one week; * * * is understood to have agreed with Judge Lawrence, when he was in Washington on duty connected with the Louisiana commission, that if any agreement was made in reference to this matter it should be kept."

Tribune, May 12, p. 1.

"Judge Lawrence will have an interview with Senator Sherman to-morrow if he returns, and with the President."

Tribune, May 22, p. 1.

"Secretary Sherman declines to issue a positive order for the dismissal of the suit against Jacob Rehm, the leader of the Chicago whiskey conspirators. He will leave it to the court to determine * * * whether the honor and good faith of the Government require that the prosecution should be discontinued. If the court shall so decide, the district attorney will be directed to dismiss the suit. * * * This is a question of which, before this decision by the Secretary, the court would have no jurisdiction."

Closing Note.

Jake Rehm has since been entirely released. The Department dared not do it directly and did it by subterfuge, and thereby recognized Judge Lawrence for striking down Packard by subterfuge, which the Administration had not dared do directly. What Judge Lawrence realized can be ascertained when he makes known what Jake Rehm paid him.

Gen. Hawley was offered the appointment of commissioner to the Paris Exposition, and declined it because it was not pay enough; Mr. McVeagh was offered three appointments, but declined on the ground that nothing but the English mission would be compensation for his services to the Administration in procuring "local self-government" in Louisiana. All the commissioners were illegally paid their expenses from Government money, or money borrowed by Secretary Sherman, without right, from a New York bank.

W. E. C.

LETTER

WILLIAM LLOYD GARRISON

TO

WM. E. CHANDLER.

BOSTON, *January* 21, 1878.

DEAR SIR: I am indebted to you for a copy of your
letter (in pamphlet form) to the Republicans of New
Hampshire, as a member of the Republican National Committee, on "the so-called Southern policy of the adminis-
" tration of President Hayes." Having given it a careful
perusal, I avail myself of this opportunity to express my
hearty approval of it, alike as to the justness of its im-
peachment, the conclusiveness of its evidence, and the pro-
priety and pertinency of its publication in this new crisis
of our national history.

It may be safely affirmed that there has been no political
somersault so sudden, so inconsistent, or so indefensible
as that which has been made by the Republican party under
the misleading of President Hayes. In sanctioning his
Southern policy, it has undeniably gone back upon its
patriotic record; virtually admitted that the administra-
tive action of President Grant toward the South (always
approved by the party till the election of Hayes) was arbi-
trary, illegal, oppressive, as constantly asseverated by the
rebel leaders at the South, and their Northern Democratic
allies; and has credulously accepted, as a wise and concil-
iatory measure, full compliance with the factious demands
of those who are neither loyal in spirit, nor just in purpose, nor to any extent trustworthy in their promises, and
against whom the blood of thousands of murdered victims

38

of their wrath and cruelty cries to heaven for righteous
retribution.

How flagrant is the abandonment of the solemnly-re-
corded principles and pledges of the Republican party
under the new *régime* is clearly set forth in your letter.
For example, the National Republican Convention at Cincinnati, which put in nomination Rutherford B. Hayes for
the Presidency, made this a part of its platform:

" We declare it to be the SOLEMN OBLIGATION of the legislative and *executive* departments of the Government to put
in *immediate exercise* all their constitutional powers   *   *
for securing to every American citizen complete liberty
and exact equality in the exercise of all civil, political, and
public rights. To this end we IMPERATIVELY DEMAND a
Congress and *Chief Executive* whose courage and fidelity
to these duties SHALL NOT FALTER until these results are
placed beyond dispute or recall."

In accepting his nomination, Governor Hayes emphatically said:

" What the South needs most is peace, and PEACE DE-
PENDS UPON THE SUPREMACY OF THE LAW. *There can be no
enduring peace if the constitutional rights of any portion
of the people are habitually disregarded.*"

This was the one vital, all-absorbing issue of the Presidential campaign, and no one was more solicitous for
its vigorous presentation at all Republican gatherings than
Gov. Hayes. There was no difference of sentiment on
this subject among the Republican leaders, orators, or
journalists. They gave no heed to the satanic outcries
about " waving the bloody shirt," and " bayonet rule," but
carried the country by fearlessly meeting the issue upon
its merits.

To show where Gov. Hayes stood at the close of the
campaign, you effectively quote (and it cannot be quoted
too often) what he pathetically declared when it was at
first supposed, from the reported but unverified electoral
returns, that he had lost his election:

" I do not care for myself, * * * * *but I do care for* the poor colored men of the South. * * * Northern men cannot live there, and will leave. * * * *The Southern people will practically treat the constitutional amendments as nullities,* and then *the colored man's fate will be worse than when he was in slavery.* * * * That is the only reason I regret that the news is as it is."

Was there a solitary man, North or South, who drew any other inference from such compassionate and regretful language than that, if his election to the Presidency had been made sure, Gov. Hayes would have promptly extended to the class with whom he professed to sympathize so profoundly the necessary means and methods of Federal protection? Were not Governors Chamberlain and Packard, with their Republican Legislatures, fully justified in believing that their rightful claim to be recognized as the legitimate authorities in South Carolina and Louisiana would have been sanctioned and upheld? Marvellous inconsistency! With no change of circumstances whatever, with the same obligations resting upon him to be faithful to his high trust, as soon as he got fairly seated in the Presidential chair, he proceeded to do exactly what his Democratic opponent (if elected) would have done, and all that he could have done—namely, withdraw the Federal troops—and thus "leave the poor colored people of the " South," and also all the loyal white Republicans, "with-" out any protection!" Yet it was solely by the presence of those troops, by " bayonet rule," that his election was carried in South Carolina, Louisiana, and Florida, without whose votes no Electoral Commission could have recorded its verdict in his favor. Assuredly, his title to the Presidency is no more valid than was that of Chamberlain and Packard to the offices they filled; and as he was instrumental in causing their expulsion therefrom, and putting two audacious " shot-gun " usurpers, Hampton and Nicholls, in their places, he has vitiated his own title, and (measuring him by his own rule) opened the way for contesting his right to be President, the decision of the Electoral Commission to the contrary notwithstanding. The

Democratic allegation of "fraud," in his case, is thus rendered more than plausible; and the only reason why there will probably be no serious attempt to effect his ejectment is, that his "Southern policy" is all that the rebel Democratic party has contended for from the beginning.

How shall this sudden and astounding "change of base" be accounted for ? You undertake to show, both by direct and circumstantial evidence, that it was made in fulfilment of a bargain entered into during the Presidential count, by representative persons on both sides, "; that the count should " not be broken up in the House, but that Hayes should " be declared and inaugurated President," provided he would withdraw the troops from South Carolina and Louisiana, and thus secure the recognition of the governments of Wade Hampton and F. H. Nicholls in those States You have made out a very strong *prima facie* case. It is not material, however, whether any such bargain was actually made or subscribed in due form, as in all probability it was not, or whether there was only a tacit but *bona fide* understanding between the contracting parties that such would be the action of Mr. Hayes, if the Electoral Commission should decide the case in his favor—its decision to be regarded as final. It suffices to know that the troops were withdrawn, President Hayes being fully aware that the immediate result of his order would be the overthrow of the legally-constituted authorities, and the seizure of the reins of government by as desperate a band of conspirators as can be found in the annals of human criminality. For the official recognition of the former, forsooth, the President could find no constitutional warrant; but only for the latter, which recognition he was as prompt in making as they were in usurping trusts and powers never committed to them by the people! "To this complexion it " has come at last;" and this turning of things upside down—this aiding a factions but powerful minority, organized and equipped with shot-guns and revolvers, to accomplish their nefarious designs against an unquestionable majority—we are called upon to sanction and admire as statesmanship of the first order! Whoever says nay, let him be *anathema maranatha!* The President, we are told, sits in his magisterial chair, serene, smiling, complacent, and confident that the best way to protect sheep from being devoured is to give them over to the custody of the wolves, withdrawing both shepherd and watch-dog as inciting to slaughter, and rendering " conciliation " impracticable by their presence! The Southern conspirators are jubilant; their Northern Democratic allies are equally elated; and credulous, hood-winked, temporizing Republicans affect to be equally delighted! Is it not time seriously to ask, " From whence doth this union arise ? " These parties may continue vociferously to sing—

> " Lo! what an entertaining sight
> Are brethren who agree! "

But the entertainment is none the less an abomination, and the agreement is but a renewal of the old " covenant with " death."

It is not surprising that the defenders of the President are involved in glaring inconsistency. First, they laud him to the skies for originating a new " policy," which, it is claimed, will render everything halcyon at the South, stop the effusion of blood, and insure protection for all classes in the exercise of their civil and political rights. But should it prove unavailing, then it can and will be changed; for, has not the President repeatedly intimated as much ? But how changed ? By substituting " bayonet rule " once more ? But they deny his right to use this power, and he has closed the door so that he cannot enter it if he would; for no appeal for Federal interposition will be made where no Republican Governor or Legislature is allowed to exist, and so all manner of atrocities may be perpetrated with impunity upon the defenceless colored population and their white sympathizers. Yes, by this " policy," four millions of loyal, native-born citizens are abandoned to their fate, and have nothing to depend upon for succor or protection but the " tender mercies " of their old oppressors. What if all the foreign-born Irish or Germans—neither of them more numerous in the aggregate—were to be ruthlessly despoiled of their rights, and reduced to a state of vassalage, after being admitted to citizenship, would not the land be convulsed as if an earthquake had shaken it from centre to circumference? Personal rights and constitutional guarantees are not matters of governmental "policy," but to be maintained against any combination that may factiously plot for their destruction.

But we are complacently told that this wonderful "policy" has brought quietude to South Carolina and Louisiana, the shot-gun is laid aside, and blood no longer flows. Well, "order reigns in Warsaw," but where is Poland? They who are in their graves excite no animosities. The colored people of those States have, by this process, been thoroughly "bull-dozed;" their spirits are broken, their hopes blasted, their means of defence wrested from them: what need of killing or hunting them any longer? And is this awful state of things to be held up as something worthy of congratulation? To talk of "conciliation" and "peace" purchased at such a price and by such base devices is an outrageous perversion of language, and an insult to the human understanding. But it is not true that acts of violence and cruelty have ceased to be perpetrated, though *pro tempore* they are lessened. There is, however, no provocation at present for a renewal of those murderous political raids by which so many loyal white and colored citizens have been driven from their homes, hunted like wild beasts, and savagely put to death. Wait until the return of another State or Presidential election, and then, if these dreadful tragedies are not re-enacted, it will be solely because all loyal assertion of citizenship at the polls has been effectually crushed.

> " Yet laugh not in your carnival of crime
> Too proudly, ye oppressors " !

There is coming a day of reckoning; and with what measure ye mete, it shall be measured to you again! The divine promise shall yet be fulfilled to the letter: "For " the oppression of the poor, for the sighing of the needy, " now will I arise, saith the Lord; I will set him in safety " from him that puffeth at him."

Next, we are told that President Hayes, in withdrawing the troops, was simply performing his constitutional duty; for there was no existing violence to require their presence. If this were so, what sense is there in eulogistically descanting upon his "policy," and claiming for it rare wisdom in its inception and execution ? Trying an experiment is one thing; discharging an imperative official obligation is another. The two are not interchangeable. President Hayes was elected, not to act the part of an experimentalist, not to "conciliate" rank sedition, but faithfully to administer the government in accordance with his oath. He is, therefore, absurdly taking credit to himself, and those who sustain his action are as absurdly bestowing it upon him, for devising nothing, inasmuch as his much vaunted "policy of conciliation" turns out to be purely mythical ! Either horn of the dilemma is sufficient for his and their impalement.

But how utterly at variance with all the facts in the case is the assertion that there was no such "domestic violence" in South Carolina and Louisiana as to justify Federal interposition ! Those bandits, the White Leaguers and Ku-Kluxes, were thoroughly armed, organized, and drilled to put down the lawfully-elected State governments, to the shedding of any amount of blood if necessary, as soon as the troops should be withdrawn ; and for months they had prevented the enforcement of law and order. It was still a reign of terror universally. Disloyalty was in the ascendant, and loyalty in the dust. The assassination of Governors Chamberlain and Packard was imminent from hour to hour. The atmosphere was "hot with flame," and the passions of the lawless populace were at a white heat.

It was under these circumstances, and knowing what would follow, that President Hayes ordered the withdrawal of the troops. They had been properly sent there by President Grant, legally and in accordance with the requirements of the United States Constitution, and the emergency that demanded their presence had not passed away. But President Hayes should have promptly done what President Grant inconsistently failed to do—recog-

nized the legitimacy of the Republican administration in
each of those States—in which case the plotters of sedition
would have been cowed into submission, for they have no
stomach to measure weapons again with the American
Government. This "the poor colored people," whose desperate situation he affected to deplore in case of Tilden's
election, had a right to expect, and did confidently expect,
at his hands, as well as all the loyal white population.
Put Tilden in the Presidential chair, he said, and "North-
"ern men cannot live at the South, and will leave. The
"Southern people will practically treat the constitutional
"amendments as nullities, and then the colored man's fate
"will be worse than when he was in slavery." How he stands
condemned out of his own mouth! How he has broken
all his oft-repeated pledges of protection to those who, to
secure his election, heroically encountered terrible sufferings and deadly perils in getting to the polls, many of
them being maimed, and others killed outright! And then
to remember what he said at Atlanta to the rebel whites
who were cheering him vociferously: "With no discredit
"to you, and no special credit to us, the war turned out as
"it did!" And again: "You joined the Confederate side
"and fought bravely, risked your lives heroically in behalf
"of your convictions"—i. e., in behalf of a treasonable
overthrow of constitutional liberty, and the establishment
of a slaveholding empire upon its ruins! Then, turning
to those of another complexion, he enticingly said: "And
"now, my colored friends, listen! After thinking it over,
"[mark his deliberation,] I believed that your rights and
"interests would be safer if the great mass of intelligent
"white men were LET ALONE by the General Government!"
But not one of those men had been interfered with by the
Government, except to put a stop to murder and assassination; and if "the great mass" had been held in unwilling
restraint by it, it proves conclusively that they had perpetrated or encouraged these monstrous crimes. No marvel,
therefore, in order that they might continue to do so without check or limitation, like the indwelling demons of the

obsessed in the days of Jesus, all they desired was to be "LET ALONE."

Can any plea of "honesty of intentions," or "purity of motives," or a wish to see whether leviathan could be drawn out with a hook, avail aught in view of such flagrant tergiversation?

Finally, an attempt is made to dismiss this gravest of all questions from further consideration, by saying that "what "is done is done, and it is a waste of breath to prolong the "discussion." The very reverse of this is the truth. In proportion to the far-reaching consequences of a dangerous precedent is the duty to testify against it, to endeavor to bring down upon it an avalanche of popular reprobation, to refuse to accept it as a finality, to sound a tocsin of alarm to awake the slumbering, startle the indifferent, reclaim the wandering, and rally the true and good to the field of conflict for a final onset.

Those who cry "peace, peace," when there is no peace, are the real mischief-makers and fomentors of strife. Conciliation, purchased by subserviency to the vile, and at the expense of justice, means "sowing wind and reaping whirlwind." The South is still rebellious at heart though wearing the mask of submission. She has within her borders all the elements of deadly strife, ready to explode at any moment. She persistently and "practically treats the constitutional amendments as nullities," except actually re-enslaving her emancipated bondmen; and these she is endeavoring to reduce to a state of vassalage scarcely less tolerable. There is no liberty of speech or of the press on her soil, except to pander to her pride and glorify her "confederate" uprising. She cares nothing for the flag, the Constitution, or the Union, beyond making them subordinate to her own sectional purposes. This is the curse that cleaves to her, like the poisoned shirt of Nessus, and enters into her blood and bones and marrow; it distorts her vision, perverts her judgment, corrupts her heart, inflames her spirit. Heaven's righteous retribution for her long-continued cruelty and oppression!

Lamentable is it that the Republican party, in order not

to break with the President of its choice, abandons the
ground upon which it has won all its laurels :

> "Massachusetts—God forgive her !—she's a-kneeling with the
> rest !"

Yes, the most subservient of them all ! Happily, there are
very many in its ranks who are too strong in their integrity
to be bribed, too clear in their vision to be duped, too reso-
lute in purpose to be turned backward, too independent in
spirit to be won to silence, by any such device to placate
what is implacable, and by unwarrantable concession to
enable the Southern leaders in the Rebellion again to hold
mastery over the nation. No vote of theirs for Rutherford
B. Hayes would have been cast if they had dreamed that
his elevation to the Presidency would require implicit approval of all his measures. It will be their patriotic aim
to bring back the party to the vantage-ground it occupied
so successfully in the last Presidential struggle—*maintaining the same principles and meeting the same issues which
made it victorious*—the abandonment of which will inevi-
tably insure its ignominious defeat in the coming contest
for supremacy. *In hoc signo vinces.* The question of
liberty and equal rights, to be protected in every part of the
land, is still paramount to every other—civil service reform, finance, &c., being subordinate, however relatively
important.

> "Banks and tariffs, stocks and trade,
>   Let them rise or let them fall ;
> Freedom asks our common aid—
>   Rally one and all !"

Your letter to the Republicans of New Hampshire is a
judicial presentation of the facts in the case—a faithful
reminder of pledges sacredly made, and shamefully broken.
It can be answered only by gross misrepresentation and
passionate abuse. For publishing it you have been assailed
in the most vindictive manner by those to whose commendation you are entitled, but who have weakly surrendered to the enemy the staff of accomplishment. Their
angry excitement is the measure of their dereliction. All
that you have done for the Republican cause goes for

nothing. Now, of course, you are a disappointed office-seeker. You are conceited, factious, impertinent. Your motives are thoroughly selfish. You are "altogether a " sorry sort of person, a little trickster," and therefore of no account. True, it is graciously conceded that, in the abstract, any Republican has the right to judge for himself as to the consistency or wisdom of the President's measures ; but if he dares publicly to express his dissent, especially as to "MY policy," he must be prepared for any amount of personal detraction.

In all my political observation for more than half a century, I do not recollect when or where there has been evinced such a disposition to compel, by browbeating, a servile acquiescence in whatever course the President chooses to mark out for himself. See what vials of wrath and scurrility have been poured upon Senator Conkling, not because he has publicly uttered any disapproval of the Southern policy, but because he has not openly commended it with the zeal of a partisan ! " The head and front of his offend- " ing hath this extent—no more." Even silence and passivity are treated with the bitterest invectives. You have recorded your dissent in a manly way, and can you expect to be dealt with more leniently ? Whatever may be the opprobrium heaped upon you, allow me to share it with you.

Yours to uphold the standard,

WM. LLOYD GARRISON.

SOUTH CAROLINA JUSTICE.

THOSE WHO MURDERED NEGROES FORGIVEN, AND THOSE WHO
SERVED THE REPUBLICAN PARTY CONDEMNED WITHOUT
HAVING FAIR TRIALS.

To the Editor of The Tribune:

SIR: Will you allow me a hearing in relation to those
persecuted and prosecuted Republicans of South Carolina
whom *The Tribune* encouraged to stand firm while the
electoral vote of the State should be counted for Hayes and
Wheeler, but for whom it has no words of cheer, nor even
demands justice and a fair trial at the hands of Wade
Hampton and his officials, to whose honor and tender mercies they were committed by the policy of an Administration, to place which in power they had been urged to risk,
and did risk, their reputations and their lives?

After the United States flag was hauled down in South
Carolina by arrangement with the rebel bankrupt, Wade
Hampton, twice a traitor in arms—once in 1861, conquered,
a second time in 1877, defiant and triumphant—there were
in the State, liable to criminal punishment:

1. Alleged dishonest Republican officials, subject to the
rebel State courts.

2. Undoubted negro-murderers, who killed their victims
solely to prevent Hayes from being President, and were
therefore amenable to Federal laws and process.

HOW THE NEGRO-MURDERERS HAVE BEEN TREATED.

The negro murderers were promptly forgiven. The South
Carolina rebel legislature memorialized President Hayes to
grant them amnesty. The response was as follows:

" To Governor WADE HAMPTON:

" I am informed by the Attorney-General that he has instructed the district attorney of South Carolina to prepare
for trial only three indictments in the Ellenton case, and to

notify the parties in all other cases that they need not prepare for trial. It is possible that only one case will be tried. The indictments were found by a grand jury composed of both political parties, which seems to justify the assumption that the prosecutions are not partisan. I agree with you that a general amnesty should extend to all political offences, except those which are of the gravest character.

"R. B. HAYES.

"WASHINGTON, D. C., *May* 12, 1877."

There were no political offenders then under indictment in South Carolina, that I am aware of, except for murders of Hayes Republicans, and what of those can be considered as not of the gravest character, I cannot conceive, unless possibly those where the chivalric Southerner has refrained from mutilating the bodies! With such a letter as this before the Southern juries there was as little possibility of any conviction by a Southern jury of the high-toned butchers of Hamburg and Ellenton as there was of convicting Jefferson Davis of treason after Horace Greeley had signed his bail bond and Andrew Johnson had employed eminent counsel not to prosecute him. To make immunity and amnesty more sure, however, when the unhanged South Carolina traitor returned from his Northern tour, where he had been introduced as that " great and good man, Wade Hampton," he carried with him, as a parting donation of peace and conciliation, the appointment, as United States district attorney, of a renegade Republican and assistant Democrat, one Northrop, who proceeded to select as his assistant a bitter Democrat ; and thereupon the South Carolina murderers, who should have been tried in the dock, became the masters of the United States courts, and the amnesty promised to Wade Hampton was fulfilled.

HOW ACCUSED REPUBLICANS HAVE BEEN TREATED.

While complete amnesty, security, and political power to butchers of Republicans have thus been obtained, what steps have been taken by the Administration or any Northern Republicans to secure a fair trial to the accused South Carolina Republicans, upon whom Wade Hampton and his infuriated blood-hounds have turned with savage ferocity? A Congressman has been dragged from Washington and convicted and incarcerated; two Republican officials have been sentenced and imprisoned, and a United States Senator is threatened with a similar fate. Are these things being fairly done? Are the accused having fair trials? Are they being prosecuted solely from a love of justice and according to a correct administration of the criminal laws, and not as measures of political persecution, revenge, and ferocity? If they are, nothing need be said nor can be done about it; but if not, the Republicans of the North need to give the subject careful investigation, and to take manly and courageous action.

It may be an unpopular work to say anything in seeming defence of " carpet-bag Republicans accused of thievery and rascality ;" it is undoubtedly easier for Northern Republicans to turn to them a deaf ear, to say that they are a bad lot, and to let Wade Hampton and his ministers of justice (!) convey them speedily into the penitentiaries. But such is not the duty of the Republican party, nor of *The Tribune.* Whatever these men have done, they are entitled to fair trials. Are they having them? If not, they should be secured for them, or those Republicans who are enjoying emoluments and high honors obtained for them in part by the fidelity and courage of these men, now betrayed, surrendered, accused, and in peril, should return their thirty pieces of silver, and go and hang themselves.

I undertake to say that the South Carolina Republicans, now pursued by that "great and good man," Wade Hampton, and his Attorney-General, Conner, are not having fair trials. The convictions are being secured by means of a political crusade and campaign, carried on by masses of infuriated Democrats, who swarm the court-houses, intimidate the witnesses and colored jurymen, and greet with applause and cheers the rendition of the verdicts of guilty. The witnesses are confessed scoundrels, granted immunity for falsely swearing into prison obnoxious Republicans and protecting Democratic thieves. Will you look at the facts in one case—that of L. Cass Carpenter?

CARPENTER'S TRIAL.

Mr. Carpenter ran for Congress last fall, has been a prominent editor, and in 1870 published *The Daily Union,* at Columbia, and edited *The Daily Republican,* at Charleston. He has been convicted and imprisoned for forgery, in altering, in 1872, an account against the State from $720 to $1,720. Here is the account:

COLUMBIA, S. C., *Dec.* 13, 1871.

Messrs. WOODRUFF & JONES,
         Clerks General Assembly,
     To *The Daily Union,*   Dr.
To publishing laws regulating insurance policies
     in daily and weekly.....................$1,720 00
     We hereby certify that the within account is correct, and remains unpaid. $1,720 00.
A. O. JONES,   J. WOODRUFF,
     Clerk H. of R.   *Clerk Senate.*
Paid on the within, Dec. 13, 1871............. ....$500
Paid on the within, Dec. 16, 1871................. 350
Paid on the within, Dec. 23, 1871................. 500
Paid on the within, Jan. 2, 1872.................. 370

J. Woodruff swore that he approved the account, and thought the figure 1 had been added before the 720 after he approved it; that he thought this because the figure 1 looked darker and heavier than the other figures; he also swore that he did not think he approved the account for so large a sum as $1,720, but he admitted that he did not examine the newspaper accounts, but approved them whenever presented, and had often approved Carpenter's bills for larger sums than $1,720, and would have approved a large as readily as a small account; that he kept no record of bills presented or approved, and could not tell whether $1,720 was due or not.

A. O. Jones testified the same as Woodruff, his testimony being the weaker of the two. Neither swore positively that the account was ever less than $1,720, and both based their judgment that the account had been altered, upon their opinion that the 1 looked darker and heavier. This was all the direct testimony of the State.

Mr. Carpenter then proved his contract with the State;

showed from the files of his paper that he had published the laws by every insertion charged for, and proved that, at the time this account was paid, the State owed him more than the amount of the account.

Upon this state of the proofs, (with an entire absence of motive for altering the bill, such motive being not merely not proved, but actually disproved,) and solely on the idea that the 1 looked as if it had been added, a South Carolina jury convicted Carpenter, and he is now imprisoned on his sentence! I will not comment on the case except to say that Woodruff and Jones, the State witnesses, are self-admitted felons, who have stolen money from the State. Woodruff admits that he raised an account from $45,000 to $90,000, and yet he is retained as clerk of the Senate, which has, by the policy of conciliation since March 4, been changed from eighteen Republicans to fourteen Democrats into a unanimously Democratic body. This is because he is a " native" thief, and if pushed will tell of Democratic frauds; so his only punishment is to swear falsely against obnoxious Republicans. By such testimony Mr. Carpenter has been convicted; not because he has been guilty, but because he has been a Republican editor and speaker, and from 1871 to this time, in *The Daily Union* and elsewhere, has exposed the Ku-Klux outrages, and has endeavored to bring their perpetrators to justice.

It is a mistake to say the investigations and trials have been fair because Republicans have been upon the committees and juries.

The Investigating Committee, whose report has been published, was composed of five Democrats, and John R. Cochran made chairman to convey the impression that the committee was Republican; but he ran as an Independent, was elected in a Democratic county, by Democratic votes. The Grand Jury was composed of virulent Democrats and a few helpless and ignorant colored men, who did not dare refuse to join in finding bills. The judge never claimed to be a Republican, although elected by a Republican Legislature. Like many other men elected by Republicans to office, he was weak and unreliable when called to protect Republicans against an infuriated public sentiment. The petit jury was composed of seven partisan Democrats and five ignorant negroes, utterly helpless before their "conciliated" white associates, and before the outside demonstrations of a determination to force convictions which have characterized these prosecutions.

But I am occupying too much of your space. If these things be, and the Republicans of the North can do nothing about them, they had better disband, as the Republican party of the South has been compelled to do. On one side we see the Confederate generals who led the rebellion taking possession of both Houses of Congress and marching toward the White House; dominating the Democratic party and shaping its policy; crushing out Republicanism and the right of suffrage at the South, and wrongfully prosecuting and imprisoning, without fair trial, American citizens. On the other side we see the Republican party, of glorious achievements, which resisted slavery extension, put down a rebellion, emancipated the colored men and gave them suffrage, and which had the courage to take the Presidency away from Samuel J. Tilden by enforcing the laws of Louisiana made for the protection of the Southern white and black Republicans, now parting with its manhood, abasing itself before Southern rebels; wrapping itself about with the garments of self-righteousness, and saying to the negro and the carpet-bagger, "We never knew you; make terms with the Democrats. We are enjoying high offices, conciliating the men from whom you wrested them, pacifying the country, and reforming the Civil Service! Grant captured John B. Gordon at Appomattox, but corrupted the Civil Service. We surrender to John B. Gordon, but we turn out Grant's corrupt appointees."

National pacification and Civil Service Reform! Please send a copy of Mr. Curtis's speech on this subject to Mrs. Emily Chisholm, Kemper county, Mississippi!

W. E. CHANDLER.

Concord, N. H., Nov. 30, 1877.

GORDON *vs.* CONKLING.

THE SENATOR FROM GEORGIA REOPENS THE DISPUTE AND SAYS THE
SENATOR FROM NEW YORK INSULTED HIM.

To the Editor of The Tribune:

SIR: A striking instance of "Southern Faith" is the
course pursued by Senator Gordon's friends since the assumed settlement of the difficulty between him and Senator
Conkling.

The paper relative to the "so-called misunderstanding"
between Senators Conkling and Gordon, while stating that
one party used the "first offensive words," decided that
there should be mutually and simultaneously withdrawn
all the remarks of both. This decision, if binding, was
clearly a waiver of the right of the party to whom the first
offensive words were spoken to require, in order to a settlement, that those words should be first withdrawn. Such
waiver clearly left no right to the party who first offended,
to publicly insist that he was first insulted by the other, and
was proceeding to notice and resent the insult and demand
satisfaction when friends intervened.

Is not this being done by Senator Gordon or his friends?
The *Washington Post* of Saturday asserts that the insults
of Conkling, systematically given to Southern Senators for
the deliberate purpose of stirring up bad blood, culminated
in executive session the day before, and then gives an account of the transaction which represents Senator Conkling
as first insulting Senator Gordon, while the latter only "re-
buked the insult" and "firmly and distinctly" repeated
his remarks. Next, the *Washington Post* of Monday has
an interview with Senator Gordon, who is represented as
saying that the account in Saturday's *Post* was precisely
accurate, and that a true account of the matter could be
obtained from his friends; and then follows an account of
an interview with a Southern Senator, who is represented
as asserting that Senator Gordon was entirely right, Sen-

55

ator Conkling in every way wrong, and that had not the matter become personal, Gordon would undoubtedly, by a large vote, have been sustained by the Senate in his position. "Senator Gordon felt that he was right; he also felt "that Mr. Conkling's remarks could be construed in no "other way than as an insult to him, and so his friends felt." This version of the facts is being spread over the whole South, and also, to a less extent, in the North.

Now, if it should be true, as I assert it is,

1. That Senator Gordon uttered the first offensive words,

2. That Senator Conkling replied in justifiable parliamentary language, and, therefore,

3. That Senator Gordon was all wrong and Senator Conkling entirely right:

Should not Senator Gordon, if responsible for the *Post's* utterances, or his friends, be requested to refrain from giving out untrue statements of the affair, and should not the correct statement be given to the world in as authentic a form as has the settlement whereby Senator Conkling has waived that which was first due to him, namely, an apology from Senator Gordon?

It is of some importance to know whether this first attempt to renew plantation manners in the Senate is to be understood as based upon the old Southern plan: "First insult your Northern man. If he resents it in any way, insist that he first insulted you, and either knock him down, shoot him on the spot, or challenge him."

W. E. CHANDLER.

WASHINGTON *Dec.* 18, 1877.

"And they all with one consent began to make excuse."

WAS IT A—

BARGAIN?

TRADE?

ASSURANCE?

AGREEMENT?

COMPACT?

CONTRACT?

COMPROMISE?

UNDERSTANDING?

OR WHAT WAS IT?

"WHAT'S IN A NAME?"

[Appendix.—February 22, 1878.]

Since the introductory note to this pamphlet was printed, various gentlemen have begun to excuse themselves concerning the so-called Louisiana bargain, which makes pertinent a review of the question.

Mr. J. A. Garfield, in the House of Representatives, February 13, referring to the Southern Democrats who resisted filibustering on the electoral count, said, (according to the *Record :*)

"If there be a man in this world who says they traded, that man has been miserably duped, or he lies."

According to the press dispatches, which profess to be verbatim:

"If there be a mortal man in this world that says they traded I believe that that man lies."

He also says: "And if there be a man in this world who says that any man on this side of the House, or the President, or anybody for the President, made a trade to secure the defeat of the filibusters, I hope he will exhibit the trade, and let the scoundrels who authorized it or made it be lashed naked through the world."

The Charge that they Traded.

The charge in Mr. Chandler's letter was in these words:

"Senator Sherman had visited Ohio, and consulted Governor Hayes. Mr. Henry Watterson, a Democratic member, and a nephew of Mr. Stanley Matthews, had acted as go-between; and on the one side, Messrs. Matthews, Charles Foster, John Sherman, James A. Garfield, and on the other, L. Q. C. Lamar, John B. Gordon, E. J. Ellis, Randall Gibson, E. A. Burke, and John Young Brown, had agreed (1) that the count should not be broken up in the House, but that Hayes should be declared and inaugurated President, and (2) that upon Hayes' accession the troops should be withdrawn from protecting Governors Chamberlain and Packard, and that the new Administration should recognize the governments of Wade Hampton in South Carolina and F. H. Nicholls in Louisiana.

"By certain general and indefinite letters since given to the public, by a secret writing now in the hands of E. A. Burke, and in other ways, the agreement was authenticated." (Page 14.)

A more detailed statement of the transactions thus briefly indicated is as follows:

I.

Mr. W. R. Roberts, of the New Orleans *Times*, had, December 3, 1876, commenced negotiating with Governor Hayes for the surrender to the rebel mobs of the Chamberlain and Packard governments, as appears by the Cincinnati *Enquirer* of that date. The accuracy of the interview as there stated was denied, but the fact of a lengthy conference admitted.

T. J. Mackey, a renegade Republican, (now rewarded by Wade Hampton for his treacherous labors by a judgeship,) had visited Governor Hayes to urge the betrayal of Chamberlain's government. Various other religious, secular, and political negotiators had interviews with Governor Hayes to satisfy him that peace and patriotism would be promoted by his taking the Presidency by the vote of Louisiana and then destroying Packard's government.

Mr. Chas. Foster, in a speech in the House, February 20, gushed over with fervent affection for Southern patriots, and proclaimed Governor Hayes' aversion to sectional parties and his determination that "the flag should float over States, not provinces—over freemen, not subjects!"

II.

The preliminary courtesies having been exchanged, the serious negotiations began. On the day of Mr. Foster's speech, Mr. Lamar wrote Mr. E. J. Ellis (page 25) that Foster said that Matthews had urged him to say squarely that Hayes would have nothing to do with or say to Packard, "because it is the truth," and Mr. Lamar urged Mr. Ellis to see Mr. Matthews at once and ask him if " President Hayes will give you some assurances that Hayes will not maintain Packard in his domination of your people." What Mr. Ellis did has not transpired, but it is certain that between that date and February 24 Senator Sherman left Washington, went to Columbus, and had consultation with President Hayes.

On the 26th of February Mr. John Young Brown and Senator Gordon made the demand which Mr. Lamar had advised Mr. Ellis to make. In the *Courier-Journal* of March 29 is a statement of Mr. John Young Brown (acknowledged by him to be correct in his recent letter dated February 1, 1878, in the *Courier-Journal* of February 2) which gives the particulars of this demand and its results. (See *post*.)

Mr. Brown said to Mr. Foster :

" If I thought that, by voting to complete the count which was to result in the inauguration of Mr. Hayes, I would be aiding * * * in perpetuating the usurpations of Packard and Chamberlain, * * * I would reverse my action, and do my very utmost to defeat the execution of the bill, regardless of consequences ; * * * that if I changed my position I knew of several prominent gentlemen who would join me, and if at that critical hour * * * the line of the Democrats who were voting to execute the law should be broken, it would result in a stampede among them, and Mr. Hayes would no more be President than he (Foster) would be."

" Mr. Foster said he believed this."

Mr. Brown continues : " I told him I had come to request of him written assurances that, if Governor Hayes was inaugurated, he would restore home-rule in the States of Louisiana and South Carolina, and that the people of these States should control their own affairs in their own way, as free from any interference by the Federal authority as the State of Ohio."

" The conversation was long and earnest. I told Mr. Foster that I wanted no bargain, no agreement; *that I scorned the thought of it;* * * * that I desired a written assurance from him that the policy of Mr. Hayes would be as indicated."

" The reply to all this was frank, full, earnest, and satisfactory to my friend, General Gordon, and myself. * * * He agreed to give me the desired letter, and said he would also request Stanley Matthews to sign it. He promised to meet me that night at my rooms. He came about midnight, and said, by reason of his interview with General Gordon and myself, he had that evening procured a meeting of some gentlemen from Louisiana and South Carolina at Wormley's Hotel, at which also the Hon. Henry Watterson was present. * * * On leaving he remarked that I should have the letter next morning."

Mr. Brown also states that the next day Mr. Foster gave him the letter signed by Matthews and himself, which he criticised as containing " some generalities " that he did not like. Mr. Foster replied that Mr. Matthews had re-written it, and added:

"Brown, it is intended to cover the whole case, and I can promise you there will be no doubt about the fulfilment of all the assurances I have given you." "I noticed the original letter on his desk, and said, 'Sign that, also,' and he replied, 'Certainly, with pleasure.'

"As I was leaving he called me back and told me that PRESIDENT GRANT WOULD, AS SOON AS THE COUNT WAS COMPLETED, ISSUE A CERTAIN ORDER TO GEN. AUGUR IN LOUISIANA. He requested me not to mention this fact for several days, but expressly gave me permission to make any use of the letter I might desire. The order referred to was issued by President Grant. I gave copies of the letters to Messrs. Levy, Ellis, and Burke, * * * and to Gen. M. C. Butler, * * with authority to use them whenever they pleased." * * * * *

"Had I believed that the policy of Mr. Hayes, if inaugurated, would not relieve them from the hateful and unrepublican supervision by the army, and the further plundering and oppression by men alien to them in birth and sympathies, I should never have voted as I did. The Hon. Charles Foster secured the inauguration of the President. EXCEPT FOR THIS SPEECH AND THESE LETTERS, THE RESULT WOULD NEVER HAVE BEEN REACHED."

The written agreement given by Mr. Foster, on February 26, as the result of his conferences with Messrs. Gordon and Brown, assured them that he was in favor of adopting "such a policy as will give the people of the States of South Carolina and Louisiana the right to control their affairs in their own way," and that he felt authorized "to pledge ourselves to you for him [Gov. Hayes] that such will be his policy."

Mr. Matthews also signed a modified form of the same pledge; "that such will be the policy of his administration." (See *post.*)

III.

These letters were kept secret from all Republicans, except a few who were engaged in the negotiations, but were shown to Democrats to induce a cessation of the filibustering which was hindering the electoral count. They were not, however, deemed sufficient by the Louisianians, who demanded more explicit and authentic guarantees. Conferences were therefore held at Wormley's Hotel, between Southern Democrats and Messrs. Matthews, Foster, Sherman, Garfield, and other Republicans, at which the surrender of the Packard government was agreed to, and at one of these conferences a written memorandum was submitted as being what was agreed to on both sides as the result of the conferences, and this memorandum provided for the withdrawal of the troops of the United States from sustaining the Packard government. It was assented to as correct, and it was proposed that it should be authenticated by signatures, but Messrs. Sherman and Garfield demurred for evident reasons, and thereupon the Southern Democrats certified to its correctness.

This certification coming to the knowledge of Mr. Garfield, he (as he has said) prepared a memorandum of his own concerning the conferences, which he now has, unless it has been destroyed. The other memorandum was retained by E. A. Burke, with the understanding that it should not be divulged unless its provisions were violated.

IV.

Even these cowardly and disgraceful pledges made by Republicans previously reputable, including a sworn member of the electoral commission then in session, trading on the result of its judgment not then finally rendered, were not fully trusted by the Louisiana Democrats, and they pressed for some performance as well as promises, and in the meantime the filibustering efforts to break up the count were continued. One of Mr. Foster's secret promises to Mr. Brown having been that a certain order should be issued by President Grant to General Augur, in Louisiana, its fulfilment was demanded. But President Grant had no doubt whatever that the Packard government (1) was honestly and legally elected, (2) had the right to distinct and unqualified recognition by the Federal Government, and (3) was entitled to the aid of the United States army to protect it and enable it to suppress the Nicholls government; and although he preferred, if events would permit, to await the opinion of Congress before taking absolutely final and decisive action, he had assured Senator Kellogg that, if the vote of Louisiana should be counted for the Hayes electors, he would fully recognize and sustain Governor Packard; and he had no idea, until authoritatively so informed, that the infamy was contemplated of taking the Presidency by the vote of Louisiana, and then, in pursuance of a prior bargain to that effect, striking down the State government elected by the same ballots and declared chosen by the same tribunal that secured the Presidential result. The bargainers were, therefore, in trouble. Their well-laid plot was in imminent danger of complete frustration by the full recognition and establishment of the Packard government by President Grant, after which his successor would not dare to destroy it. In this emergency counsel for Mr. Hayes before the Electoral Commission, particularly Mr. William M. Evarts—who, although keeping well concealed, was from the first malignantly determined to destroy the Packard government as soon as the electoral vote was safe—made earnest requests of President Grant and his Cabinet that Packard should not be recognized, but that the question should be left for his successor, and to these importunities President Grant yielded. The bargainers then pressed him to issue the order to General Augur which they had promised should be issued. This he delayed giving, and the efforts to break up the count continued up to and during the night of Thursday, March 1, when the great crisis of the Presidential struggle arrived. During the conflict in the House of Representatives over an alleged second return from Vermont, presented by Mr. A. S. Hewitt, the record shows that, on the first roll-call, Mr. E. J. Ellis voted with the filibusters, then 116 against 148; but on the next roll-call, which immediately followed, he changed and voted with the majority—147 to 115.

At this time he informed Mr. Hewitt that all was safe, and that he was satisfied. Mr. Hewitt states (Record, February 14, 1878) "that negotiations went on, and that these gentlemen from Louisiana were satisfied I do know." At the same hour Mr. Representative Wm. M. Levy, speaking on this Vermont case, (Record, March 1, 1877, page 2047,) announced that assurances had been given by friends of Mr. Hayes that the troops should be no longer used to force governments not of their choice upon the Southern States; and he called upon those members who had been influenced in their action by a desire to protect Louisiana and South Carolina to join him in voting for the completion of the count. From this time all doubt as to the result ceased, and at four in the morning of March 2 Hayes and Wheeler were declared elected.

Precisely what finally satisfied the Democratic bargainers the public do not yet know. It is fair to presume that it was either vehement assurances from the Republican traders as to what should certainly be done on the next day, or else some communication from Governor Hayes, who was that night coming on the cars through Pennsylvania, which induced Messrs. Ellis, Levy, Gibson, and other Southern defenders, advisers, and directors of the present Administration, to graciously allow Hayes to be counted in. What the actual determining assurance was is a subject worthy of investigation.

This much, however, is known: Governor Hayes reached Washington at 9.15 Friday morning, March 2, and went to the residence of Senator Sherman. Between eleven and twelve he went with General W. T. Sherman to the Executive Mansion, where the Cabinet were assembling. A consultation between Governor Hayes and President Grant, concerning Louisiana affairs, took place, and the order contracted for February 26 by Mr. Chas. Foster was authentically issued by General Sherman by advice of Governor Hayes, as follows:

HEADQUARTERS OF THE ARMY,
March 2, 1877, **12.22 P. M.**

To GEN. C. C. AUGUR:
Commanding Department of New Orleans:

The following dispatch has gone to Governor Packard, and is hereby sent you for your government and information.

W. T. SHERMAN.

The dispatch following was not even signed by President Grant, but only by his secretary, Major Sniffen, and only stated that the President would not during the remaining days of his official life use the troops to sustain or pull down either government, nor would he recognize either claimant. But the danger of the irrevocable recognition of the Packard government by the Grant Administration was over, and the Nicholls mob felt encouraged to wait until President Hayes fulfilled the balance of the contract.

The New York *Herald* correspondent, March 2, referring to the foregoing dispatches, says:

"It is understood that this action proceeded with the express agreement of Mr. Hayes made by his nearest representatives here, with his consent, and that Senator Sherman, as the chosen Secretary of the Treasury, formally agreed to this policy as to both Louisiana and South Carolina."

"Just previous to the meeting of the Cabinet to-day Messrs. Ellis and Gibson and Col. Burke of Louisiana had an extended conference with President Grant, when the latter read to them the instructions sent to Gen. Augur. Shortly after these gentlemen withdrew Messrs. Kellogg and Pitkin, representing the Packard faction, called to see the President, but he was unable to accord them an interview."

The New York *Tribune* correspondent at Washington, on March 2, says that before the Cabinet meeting that day Mr. Burke and Representatives Ellis, Gibson and Levy called on the President, and had a long interview with him. "Before they left the White House they had assurances that the promised orders to General Augur should be given."

The New York *Herald* of March 3 also gives an account of Governor Hayes' arrival in Washington and his interview with President Grant concerning the Louisiana dispatches, which resulted in General Sherman's dispatch above given.

• · *Recapitulation.*

The trade may be briefly summarized thus:

The Republicans agreed that Louisiana and South Carolina should have the right to manage their own affairs in their own way, *meaning thereby* that the Packard and Chamberlain governments should never be assisted by Federal power or recognized by the National Administration, but that the Nicholls and Hampton governments should be allowed and aided to overturn them and establish themselves, and should be recognized by the National Administration; and agreed that for the accomplishment of this purpose General Grant should be induced not to recognize the Packard government but to issue military orders to General Augur not to assist it, and that, for the same purpose, such further action should be taken by President Hayes as should become necessary.

The Democrats, in consequence of and relying upon the good faith, integrity, and truthfulness of the foregoing assurances and on the strength of these guarantees, agreed to and did resist the policy of filibustering, allowed the count to proceed, accepted the decision of the electoral commission, and acquiesced in the inauguration of the President who was counted in.

The parties who at some time in the various phases of these agreements participated therein and became responsible therefor were: Messrs. Hayes, Foster, Garfield, Sherman, Matthews, and Messrs. Brown, Gordon, Lamar, Levy, Ellis, Watterson, Burke, and others.

That the above stipulations have all been literally complied with is matter of history.

If they were not a trade, a bargain, what were they?

What Facts are in Dispute.

If the above narrative is correct, it would seem to justify the charge of a bargain as first made by Mr. Chandler. The only debatable questions are these:

WAS THERE A WRITTEN MEMORANDUM OF THE BARGAIN?

Was the agreement authenticated by a secret writing now in the hands of E. A. Burke?

In view of recent developments, this will hardly be longer denied. The New Orleans *Times* of March 7, 1877, gave an interview with Burke, who returned from Washington to New Orleans that morning, in which he states that Packard would never be recognized; that there would be but one State government, and that would be the Nicholls government; and that "WRITTEN PLEDGES HAD BEEN GIVEN," "SOLEMN AND DOCUMENTARY PLEDGES" to that effect. (See *post*.)

The New York *Tribune* of April 2, 1877, has a dispatch from Washington reporting a telegram from New Orleans, representing Burke as saying, "He has a copy of that paper, but does not feel at liberty to make its contents known;" "thinks it would be far better to publish the whole now, as the other preliminary agreements have been given to the public," and speaks of it as the "yet secret agreement to which Secretary Sherman is a party." (Page 27.)

In the Washington *Post* of February 1, 1878, Mr. Charles Foster directs an interviewer to "see Mr. A. C. Buell. I explained the whole matter in full to him, and he knows more about it than any man I can think of. Ask him about it." Mr. Buell, thus referred to, communicates to the *Post* of February 2 a long article, in which he says that "Mr. Burke drew a memorandum." "This memorandum was read at a conference at Wormley's." "Garfield is said to have made a supplementary memorandum." (See *post.*)

In a recent authorized interview with Mr. Foster in the Cincinnati *Gazette*, given in the New York *Times* of February 15, 1878, he says that at the meeting at Wormley's hotel "Mr. Burke had with him a paper, which he read to Gen. Garfield in my hearing," and that this memorandum Mr. Burke kept.

But it is needless to enlarge the proofs that there was a memorandum; after these recent admissions it cannot be seriously denied. When it suits the purposes of the bargainers, or cannot be longer withheld, it will be produced.

Yet, after the concealments, evasions, and delays that have taken place, no alleged copy that may be published will be trustworthy unless verified by the examination on oath of the parties thereto and the persons to whom it was shown.

But, although no one can state its language, nor can any copy that may be published be trusted, it is very easy to determine whether it authenticated a bargain consistent with the duties which the Republican obligors owed to their party, by referring to the description of it given by one who is reported to have seen it—Mr. Hernando D. Money, of Mississippi. In the House, March 1, 1877, just before Mr. Levy announced the bargain, Mr. Money stated his refusal to give up filibustering, notwithstanding the fair promises made as to Mr. Hayes' policy, and says:

"Knowing well that, as stated by his friends here, it traverses all the *matured utterances and carefully-considered policy and accomplished acts of his party* for the last twelve years, I must be excused from lubricating the processes of the count and hastening an event I may regret."

One point in reference to this still concealed memorandum should be noticed.

Mr. Foster, in his statement in the New York *Times* just cited, undertakes to say that the memorandum merely stated what the Nicholls government would do; treat all citizens fairly, give colored men their rights; in fact, contained substantially the declarations subsequently made by the Nicholls legislature.

Unfortunately, Mr. Foster's friend and fellow-manipulator, Mr. A. C. Buell, whom he has called in as a witness, says the memorandum recited "the Southern understanding of the scope and purport of assurances made verbally by Foster and other friends of Hayes." "The memorandum was then and there read, with the inquiry, ' Is this what you mean?' and with the reply from Hayes' friends, ' Yes, substantially!' "

A single suggestion also disposes of Mr. Foster's point about the memorandum. If it merely stated what the Nicholls government and Southern Democrats were to do, why was it retained by Burke and shown to no Republicans, but only to Democrats? Does the maker of a promissory note keep it in order to be sure that he has it to pay? If the memorandum contains promises of the Southern Democrats, Mr. Foster had better get it from Mr. Burke and see if it will not protect the Returning Board, now in the penitentiary for placing too much confidence in visiting-statesmen Sherman, Garfield, and Matthews !

WAS IT A BARGAIN?

Were the transactions which took place at the Wormley's hotel conferences and elsewhere " a bargain ?"

' All the parties to the transactions refuse to acknowledge their bantling by that name.

Was it, or not, a mutual agreement involving something to be done on each side in consideration of something to be done on the other? If so, it was most certainly a bargain.

Mr. Charles Foster (Congressional Record, Feb. 14, 1878) says it was not this. He says, " I defy mortal man to bring evidence that I pledged anybody to do anything in consequence of anything that might be done by others."

But in the same sentence Mr. Foster makes a manifest misstatement, to call it by no worse name, as appears by contrasting what he says with his published pledge.

Mr. Foster, in speech in House, Feb. 13, 1878:
"I was laboring for the execution of the compact without exacting from anybody any promises, and without *making any pledges as to what would be the policy of Mr. Hayes.*"

Mr. Foster's letter to Messrs. Brown and Gordon, Feb. 26, 1877, as to Gov. Hayes' policy concerning Louisiana and South Carolina:
"Authorized to PLEDGE ourselves to you *for him* that such will be his POLICY."

Ordinarily, against a witness thus discredited no more evidence need be adduced. But Mr. John Young Brown expressly states, as above shown, that he demanded written pledges of Mr. Foster on the ground that he could and would defeat the count unless they were given; and Mr. Brown reiterates that, if it had not been for the pledges, the inauguration of Hayes would never have been reached, and that Mr. Foster secured that result by these pledges.

Unless the correctness of this statement of Mr. Brown can be overthrown, the pretence that the pledges were not made to secure results in the House will be weak and futile. Mr. Foster, in the interview above quoted from the New York *Times* of February 15, 1878, says:

"On the 26th of February Hon. John Young Brown and Senator Gordon invited me to a conference with them, which Mr. Brown has detailed with much particularity. Some of the minor details of his statements are not in exact accordance with my remembrance of them. The final result of the interview was the promise to give him the letters signed by myself and Senator Matthews, which was done the next day, and which have been widely published. My understanding at the time was that Mr. Brown desired the letters for use in a possible contingency in the future. *Certainly no thought of influencing his action by furnishing these letters ever occurred to me.*"

This last statement is directly contradictory of Mr.

Brown's, and they cannot stand together. The latter
states that he could and would have broken up the count,
and threatened to do so unless Foster gave written assurances; and thereupon Foster gave them. Mr. Foster does
not say what was to be the future contingency in which
Mr. Brown might want to use the letters. Mr. Brown
states what he actually did with them; he gave copies to
Messrs. Levy, Ellis, and Burke, and to M. C. Butler.
" The frank, full, earnest, and satisfactory " assurances of
Mr. Foster, "and the contents of the letter were made known
to many."

" The confidence of the Democrats in him and in his authorization to say what he did composed the Representatives and caused them to remain unshaken in doing what
was right amid the storm which was raging around them,
and in the face of the earnest remonstrances of their constituents. If a few had faltered the panic would have
been general, the work of the commission would have been
fruitless, and before this time, in my opinion, a hurricane
of war would have been sweeping over the land."

All these terrible consequences, so eloquently depicted
by the young orator of Kentucky, were averted because
Mr. Charles Foster got frightened, gave one paper, gave
two papers, made earnest assurances, played the timorous
Northern doughface to rampant Southerners, and yet no
thought of influencing any one's action ever occurred to
Mr. Foster when he sunk on his knees and sold his party
and its honor!

The further contingency for which Brown wanted the
letters came. President Hayes delayed the fulfilment of
the bargain, and March 28, Mr. John Young Brown cracked
the whip from Louisville, and published the letters of
Matthews and Foster, *until then secret from Republicans*,
and demanded that Hayes should fulfil " the promises of
his friends," restore the " autonomy " of Louisiana and
South Carolina, "otherwise the whole responsibility of the
consequences, whatever they may be, will rest upon President Hayes!"

April 1, Mr. Burke, at New Orleans, followed up Brown's demand by threatening to publish the "yet secret agreement to which Secretary Sherman is a party," if not soon performed. Thereupon the bargainers at Washington hastened to prevent disclosures by announcing, April 4, Mr. Evarts' instructions to the Harlan-Hawley-McVeagh commission to go to New Orleans and trample down Packard's government, and deliver the Returning Board over to pains and penitentiaries for the sole crime of having put the bargainers in power in the White House.

No person can read attentively the documentary evidence, above recited in whole or in part, and have any lingering doubt (1) that the agreements made by Matthews and Foster meant that the Packard and Chamberlain governments should be abandoned by Hayes, and, if necessary, destroyed by him ; (2) that the agreements were made in order to prevent the breaking up of the electoral count in the House ; and (3) that they were fulfilled in order to prevent full disclosures of the disgraceful negotiations which ushered in the Administration, and are to be its eternal dishonor.

But additional evidence is not wanting that the assurances of the "friends of President Hayes" were given in order to stop filibustering and secure the completion of the count, and in consideration of these results.

Mr. Wm. M. Levy in his speech on the night of March 1st, already alluded to, distinctly declares that he calls upon his fellow-members to join him in opposing dilatory motions, by reason of the "solemn, earnest, truthful assurances" as to the policy of President Hayes.

Mr. A. S. Hewitt states in the speech above referred to :

"I had no part in the bargain, if any was made. I knew nothing of any bargain, or of its terms. But I was told on the day after the Vermont returns had been presented to the joint convention that these gentlemen from Louisiana were satisfied, *and that there was no good reason* *why the count should not proceed.* * * * * If other men made bargains I know nothing of them, but that negotiations went on, and that these gentlemen from Louisiana were satisfied, I do know, and I do know that the count was completed and the most serious complications averted." * * * * *" If it had not been that assurances were given that military domination should cease, I have reason to believe that it would never have been completed."

E. A. Burke, in the New Orleans *Times* of March 7, 1877, says that it was only on the basis of the non-recognition of Packard "that the opposition to the declaration of the election of Hayes and Wheeler in the style of filibustering was withdrawn." "The Democratic managers * * * * were not led into any trap, * * * *nor did they withdraw their opposition* until written pledges had been given."

Mr. A. C. Buell, in the Washington *Post* of February 2, in the article above cited, gives a long account, in which he says: "The Southern men accepted the honor of Charles Foster and Stanley Matthews as a guarantee for the good faith of Hayes, without collateral security (!) of any kind, and *on the strength of that guarantee* they resisted the policy of filibustering, allowed the count to proceed, accepted the decision of the Electoral Commission, and acquiesced in the inauguration of the President who was counted in." The Washington *Union* (Hayes organ) of February 4 says Buell's statements are correct.

Mr. E. John Ellis, in the House, February 13, 1878, says that any one who says that any Louisianian bartered away Mr. Tilden "lies in his heart, lies in his foul throat." But he proceeds to admit that he " began this filibustering movement, determined to defeat this great wrong" if he could, and that he attended the celebrated Wormley's-Hotel conference, and there participated in what he styles an interchange of views, but no bargain ; and he does not explain why, on the critical Vermont roll-call, he voted first with the filibusters, and immediately, on the next call, changed and voted against them, nor why, at that time, he informed Mr. Hewitt that all was right and the count could proceed. Was it some confirmatory telegram from Columbus or Pittsburg or Altoona, from the great expectant? Did he change his vote because convincing assurances had been obtained from Hayes himself securing "autonomy," or the right to butcher negroes with impunity, for Louisiana?

On one theory alone was there no bargain: that when Southern gentlemen negotiate with Northern doughfaces, the former cannot possibly become bound to the inferior class. They "scorn the idea" of a bargain with such, but compel them to give "written assurances" and trust to Southern honor!

WHAT THE BARGAINERS DESERVE.

Mr. Garfield well says that if anybody for the President made a trade to defeat the filibusters, "let the scoundrels who authorized or made it be lashed naked through the world;" and, in saying this, he pronounces his own condemnation.

Among those who participated in the trade, the most censurable are those Republicans who first went to New Orleans and urged the Louisiana Republicans to do their duty courageously, and then came to Washington and sold them out even before the vote of the State was counted for Hayes and Wheeler. Those men were Messrs Sherman, Matthews, and Garfield. They entered into intimate relations with the members of the Returning Board, and with Governors Kellogg and Packard and the other Republicans who were important to or active in the count. They showed intense anxiety for a Republican result, and aided in procuring it. Every day and hour of their long and confidential association with these Republicans were assurances that they would stand by them in whatever troubles might come to them, and conveyed pledges that if Hayes should be President he would sustain and vindicate them. During the weary hours of the winter, also, when the Returning

Board were imprisoned in Washington, extraordinary solicitude was manifested that they should stand firm, and say nothing to weaken the electoral result they had declared, but that they should watch and wait patiently till President Hayes should rescue and honor them.

But even while they were thus in prison they were deceived and betrayed. Mr. Matthews agreed, in writing, that they should be sacrificed, and wrote Packard to get out and Hayes would give him an office. Mr. Sherman, (after consulting Governor Hayes,) and Mr. Garfield, while a sworn member of the Electoral Commission, joined in bargaining away all the Republicans of Louisiana, and President Hayes participated in, confirmed, and executed the bargain.

None of them had even the decency to provide against the transfer of their dupes from the prisons of Congress to the penitentiaries of Louisiana, and there they are and will remain unless President Hayes, who abased the powers of this Government before a mob-leader, can induce him, now a usurping Governor, to pardon them. They ought to be willing to be convicted and pardoned felons in order to make Mr. Hayes President, and Mr. Sherman Secretary, and Mr. Matthews Senator, and to give to Mr. Garfield, whose Congressional career is now drawing to a close, such crumbs of office as a degraded and expiring Administration may be able to toss him, and a Democratic Senate may be induced to allow him to receive! In the hope of this he still further degrades himself by saying: " The troops were withdrawn as a matter of constitutional duty, and as such I defend the withdrawal."

When did he first announce this constitutional duty? Did he proclaim it in Louisiana during the electoral count? Did he assert it during the ensuing winter, when the Presidency trembled in the balance? Has he ever advocated it before the people of the Western Reserve ?

Or did he first learn it when bargaining with Southern Democrats at Wormley's; did he keep it secret during the Ohio canvass of last fall, when he hoped to be Senator;

and does he now for the first time disgracefully assert it to keep Southern Democrats from exposing the bargain which he and his fellow-statesmen made, and to secure a refuge for himself when the people of Ohio repudiate him as they have President Hayes, Secretary Sherman, and Senator Matthews? When he next thunders in the House, will he give a history of his conversion to the doctrine that Federal troops should not be used to protect a State government from overthrow by armed minorities?

Will he also repeat his statement of February 19 that he, upon the inauguration of Hayes, made an effort to organize a movement which, "a world of things being forgotten and forgiven on both sides," "*could put to shame the extremists on both sides*," and tell when he ceased to be an extremist and what the Republican Party has done that he begs the South to forgive, and whether his new party in Ohio was to exclude as an extremist that pioneer of Republicanism, Benjamin F. Wade, whose last days are being embittered by the treachery of Hayes and bargain of Garfield and their consequences?

But first let him and Sherman and Matthews get their poor dupes and victims out of the Louisiana prisons into which their treachery, perfidy, selfish greed, and cowardice have plunged them.

WAS GOVERNOR HAYES A BARGAINER?

A further question naturally arises and should be frankly answered: Was President Hayes a party to the bargain?

Unquestionably he was. Much of the coquetting with Southern Democrats during the winter was done by him. Messrs. Foster, Matthews, and others, kept him fully advised of what they were doing. *Senator* Sherman went to Columbus, reluctant to trade off Packard, and returned *Secretary* Sherman, and joined in the trade. Mr. Hayes knew perfectly well that the price that he was to pay for the Presidency was the betrayal of Packard and Chamberlain, and the sacrifice of his own honor; but the fear of the loss of the Presidency, with its $200,000 in money and its patronage, was too much for him, and he deliberately paid the price. It would be cowardly to affect to think otherwise. If the subject is ever investigated by competent authority it will doubtless be found that he confirmed in some way the assurances given by his friends, before Mr. Levy proclaimed in the House that all was right, and Mr. Ellis told Mr. Hewitt that the count could proceed, and changed his vote and opposed filibustering. At all events, it is enough to convict him that his first act on arriving in Washington was to procure or advise an order from General Sherman withdrawing Federal support from Packard, and inviting the White Leaguers to crush him out.

The long line of events following—

The shameless refusal to acknowledge, notice or respond to the constitutional call for Federal assistance, made March 22, by the governor and legislature of Louisiana; the hiring by Federal offices and money and the condonation of revenue frauds, of an unconstitutional commission to go to Louisiana, and destroy that governor and legislature; the order to Federal troops to retreat before a rebel mob, and the invitation to that mob to take forcible possession of Louisiana and drive into exile, or thrust into prison, the Republicans whose fidelity and courage had made him President, will degrade and disgrace Rutherford B. Hayes long after his salary of $50,000 a year has ceased to come in, and when he has nothing to do but to think how he pitied and protected the poor colored men and Republicans of the South!

A letter now lies before the writer dated February 14, 1878, from a truthful and reliable Southern Republican, who says:

"Mr. Hayes' title to the Presidency involves the blood of my brother, [shot for political reasons,] and while he luxuriates in the quiet possession of the office, with its honors and emoluments, the murderers of my brother roam at large, stimulated and encouraged by the Southern policy.

Not only this, but I and many others have since been banished from home, family, and property, persecuted and proscribed without a shadow of right, justice, or equity."

This man but echoes the sentiments of thousands of Republicans, black and white, throughout the South, who think of President Hayes and his betrayal of them, and "a curse rises unbidden to their lips."

To Republicans who, on account of Mr. Hayes' education, antecedents, and previously-estimated character, refuse to believe him deliberately guilty of causing the misery he has wrought, there is commended as a fitting description of him the words which that unsurpassed delineator of human character, George Eliot, makes her heroine Romola speak concerning Tito Melema:

"There was a man to whom I was very near, so that I could see a great deal of his life, who made almost every one fond of him, for he was young and clever and beautiful, and his manners to all were gentle and kind. I believe when I first knew him he never thought of doing anything cruel or base. But because he tried to slip away from everything that was unpleasant, and cared for nothing else so much as his own safety, he came at last to commit some of the basest deeds, such as make men infamous. He denied his father, and left him to misery; he betrayed every trust that was reposed in him that he might keep himself safe and get rich and prosperous. Yet calamity overtook him."

W. E. CHANDLER.

February 22, 1878.

ADDITIONAL PROOFS

OF THE

LOUISIANA BARGAIN.

John Young Brown's Statement.

In the New York *Tribune* of March 29, 1877, is the following:

LOUISVILLE, KY., *March 28.*—To-morrow's *Courier-Journal* will contain an interview with the Hon. John Young Brown, of Kentucky, who says:

"Herewith I publish the letters of the Hon. Charles Foster and Stanley Matthews, addressed to the Hon. John B. Gordon, and myself. The circumstances attending their origin are in brief as follows: On the 26th of February last I sent a page from the House of Representatives to the Senate Chamber for my distinguished friend General Gordon, and he came over in a few moments. I told him that I wanted an interview with the Hon. Charles Foster at which I desired his presence. I outlined to General Gordon what I intended to say to Mr. Foster, and he said he would with pleasure accompany me.

"We found Mr. Foster in the room of the Committee on Appropriations. No one else was present during the interview. I told Mr. Foster that I had, as he knew, been voting against all dilatory motions, and had in a speech advocated the inflexible execution of the Electoral bill. I had stated in a Democratic caucus that I would so vote if I were the only man from the South to do so; that the vote was approved by my judgment; that I felt under an obligation of honor to stand by the result, bitter as it was, feeling that the situation was not chargeable to the Electoral bill, but to the majority of the commission, which we had agreed to trust. I told him I had received dispatches and letters from home, from cherished and trusted friends, conveying most emphatic remonstrance against my course; but that, with my convictions about the question, if a petition signed by every voter in my district should be sent to me requesting me to support the dilatory motions, it would not alter my purpose by a hair.

"I further said to him that there was only one thing which would change me, and that was, if I thought that by voting to complete the count which was to result in the inauguration of Mr. Hayes I would be aiding directly or indirectly in perpetuating the usurpations of Packard and Chamberlain in the States of Louisiana and South Carolina, I would reverse my action and do my very utmost to defeat the execution of the bill, regardless of consequences, calamitous to the country as I believe they would be. I furthermore told him that if I changed my position I knew of several prominent gentlemen who would join me, and if at that critical hour, when the daily and nightly scenes surpassed by far the wild excitement and violence anything ever witnessed in the legislative history of the country, the line of the Democrats who were voting to execute the law should be broken, it would result in a stampede among them, and Mr. Hayes would no more be President than he (Foster) would be.

"Mr. Foster said he believed this.

"I have the highest respect for Charles Foster; I believe him to be an honorable gentleman, and I told him that it was my confidence in him that brought me to him; he represented the district of Governor Hayes; he has just made a manly and patriotic speech, in which he had said that under President Hayes, if inaugurated, the flag should float over States, not provinces: over freemen, not subjects. I referred to this speech, and told him I had come to request of him written assurances that if Governor Hayes was inaugurated President he would restore home-rule in the States of Louisiana and South Carolina, and that the people of these States should control their own affairs in their own way, as free from any intervention by the Federal authority as the State of Ohio.

"This conversation was long and earnest. I told Mr. Foster that I wanted to make no bargain, no agreement; that I scorned the thought of it; that I had declined a re-election to Congress; was voluntarily withdrawing from political life; wanted no office that a President could give me, and that my object was unselfish, and that I desired a written assurance from him that the policy of Mr. Hayes would be as indicated, and from him specially by reason of his very intimate relations with Gov. Hayes.

"The reply to all this was frank, full, earnest, and satisfactory to my friend, Gen. Gordon, and myself. Indeed, Mr. Foster said he had a letter in his pocket, just received from Gov. Hayes, thanking him for the speech to which I have alluded, and endorsing it. He offered this letter to Gen. Gordon and myself to read, but we declined it. He agreed to give me the desired letter, and said he would also request Stanley Matthews to sign it. He promised to meet me that night at my rooms. He came about midnight, and said by reason of his interview with Gen. Gordon and myself he had that evening procured a meeting of some gentlemen from Louisiana and South Carolina at Wormley's hotel, at which also the Hon. Henry Watterson was present. At the conclusion of the conference these gentlemen had expressed great satisfaction at what had been said to them. On leaving he remarked that I should have the letter next morning.

"On the next day he came to my desk, in the House of Representatives, and handed me an unsigned letter. I read it, took my pen and erased one paragraph, and told him that it could be made fuller and stronger, but that from the honorable men, who gave it in good faith, it was sufficient. In an hour afterward I went to his desk and he delivered me a letter signed by himself and Mr. Matthews. I observed that it was in a different handwriting, read it hastily, and remarked to him that it contained some generalities I did not like. He replied that Mr. Matthews had rewritten it, and added: 'Brown, it is intended to cover the whole case, and I can promise you there will be no doubt about the fulfilment of all the assurances I have given you.' I noticed the original letter on his desk, and said: 'Sign that also;' and he replied: 'Certainly, with pleasure.' As I was leaving he called me back and told me that President Grant would, as soon as the count was completed, issue a certain order to General Augur in Louisiana. He requested me not to mention this fact for several days; but expressly gave me permission to make any use of the letter I might desire. The order referred to was issued by President Grant. I gave copies of the letters to Messrs. Levy, Ellis, and Burke, of Louisiana, and to General M. C. Butler, of South Carolina, with authority to use them whenever they pleased.

"When I saw that the Democratic victory, so fairly won, was lost, my deepest concern was for my suffering Southern countrymen. To contribute to their deliverance from bondage was the passionate aspiration of my heart. Had I believed that the policy of Mr. Hayes, if inaugurated, would not relieve them from the hateful and unrepublican supervision by the army, and the further plundering and oppression by men alien to them in birth and sympathies, I should never have voted as I did. The Hon. Charles Foster secured the inauguration of the President.

"Except for this speech and these letters, the result would never have been reached. The conversation and contents of the letter were made known to many. The confidence of Democrats in him and in his authorization to say what he did co posed the Representatives, and caused them to remain unshaken in doing what they believed was right amid the storm which was raging around them, and in the face of the earnest remonstrances of their constituents. If a few had faltered the panic would have been general; the work of the Commission would have been fruitless, and before this time, in my opinion, a hurricane of war would have been sweeping over the land.

"Hope deferred has sickened the heart of Southern men. I do not understand, nor do I appreciate, the delay of President Hayes. He should not hesitate; the whole country expected the great and good work at his hands. Passionate men are heaping invectives upon the heads of those Democrats who voted to stand by the Electoral bills. This pains me, but causes no regret for my action.

"In conclusion, I will say that I have full faith in the fulfilment of the assurances contained in the letters of Messrs. Foster and Matthews. They are honorable men. I cannot believe that they would attempt deliberate deception. They are the intimate friends of the President. They know his views, and expressed them in these letters. An honest construction of their language means that the autonomy of Louisiana and South Carolina should be restored. It is impossible that the President, under all the circumstances and in view of his own utterances and the promises of his friends, can refuse at once to make Louisiana and South Carolina as free as Ohio, and have the flag float over States, not provinces; over freemen, not subjects.

"If done, the peace and prosperity of the Republic will be secured · if not done, the whole responsibility of the consequences, whatever they may be, will rest upon President Hayes.

"JOHN YOUNG BROWN."

The Letters.

House of Representatives,
Washington, D. C., *February* 26, 1877.

Gentlemen: Refering to the conversation had with you yesterday in which Governor Hayes' policy as to the status of certain Southern States was discussed, we desire to say in reply that we can assure you in the strongest possible manner of our great desire to have adopted such a policy as will give to the people of the States of South Carolina and Louisiana the right to control their own affairs in their own way; and to say further that we feel authorized, from an acquaintance with and knowledge of Governor Hayes and his views on this question, to pledge ourselves to you for him that such will be his policy.

CHARLES FOSTER.

To the Hon. John Young Brown and John B. Gordon.

—

Washington, *February* 27, 1877.

Gentlemen: Referring to the conversation had with you yesterday, in which Gov. Hayes' policy as to the status of certain Southern States was discussed, we desire to say that we can assure you in the strongest possible manner of our great desire to have him adopt such a policy as will give to the people of the States of South Carolina and Louisiana the right to control their own affairs in their own way, subject only to the Constitution of the United States and the laws made in pursuance thereof, and to say further that, from an acquaintance with and knowledge of Gov. Hayes and his views, we have the most complete confidence that such will be the policy of his administration. Respectfully,

STANLEY MATTHEWS,
CHARLES FOSTER.

To the Hon. John B. Gordon and the Hon. John Young Brown.

THE BURKE MEMORANDUM.

The existence of the Burke memorandum is stated by Mr. Burke in the following interview in the New Orleans *Times* of March 7, 1877:

"On Wednesday morning Major E. A. Burke * * * returned home, and was interviewed by a *Times* reporter. * * * Mr. Burke said he was perfectly satisfied * * * that there would be but one State government, and that would be the Nicholls government. As stated in Saturday night's telegram, Major Burke, on that evening, after President Hayes had been sworn in, held *an interview with the President at the residence of John Sherman.* * * *

"As to the recognition of the Packard government, Major Burke is fully satisfied that such a recognition will never come. * * * The commitment to that policy was made by those leading Republicans before the presidential question was settled by the House of Representatives, and it was only on that basis that the opposition to the declaration of the election of Hayes and Wheeler, in the style of filibustering, was withdrawn.

"The Democratic managers * * * were not * * * led into any trap, * * * nor did they withdraw their opposition until WRITTEN PLEDGES HAD BEEN GIVEN by those then in a position to and authorized to speak; and, since that time, those pledges have been confirmed in a most substantial manner by the same parties, and not those alone, but others.

"Whatever may have been said as to Mr. Stanley Matthews, Chas. Foster, the Hon. John Sherman, and others, having authority to speak for President Hayes, Major Burke is satisfied, from personal experience and observation, that they did have that authority, and it is quite probable that his assertion will be verified soon. * * *

"That President Hayes does not contemplate immediate action in the Louisiana case Major Burke does not deny, but, as stated above, he has the SOLEMN AND DOCUMENTARY PLEDGES of the best and the highest authority to substantiate his ideas."

There being delay in carrying out the bargain, Mr. Burke threatens to produce the paper, in an interview in the New York *Tribune* of April 2, contained on page 27 of this pamphlet, and, two days after, the instructions were issued to the Harlan commission to destroy the Packard legislature. (Page 28.)

In the Washington *Post* of February 1 is an interview with Mr. Chas. Foster, in which he admits a conference at Wormley's Hotel with Mr. Henry Watterson, E. John Ellis, John Sherman, Stanley Matthews, General Garfield, E. A. Burke, and others, and that Mr. Burke read a paper at that conference.' Mr. Foster then proceeds: "See Mr. A. C. Buell: I explained the whole matter in full to him, and he knows more about it than any man I can think of. Ask him about it."

In the *Post* of February 2, Mr. A. C. Buell communicates, in a long article, his views as to the understanding between Mr. Foster and other Republicans, and the Southern Democrats.

Referring to the letter of Gov. Hayes to Mr. Foster, he says:

"The text of the letter was circulated, and the Southern men held several informal conferences at various places. the net result of which was the conference at Wormley's, between those Southern Democrats and those friends of Hayes whose names Mr. Foster mentioned in the interview printed yesterday." * * * "There were many conferences, all informal, and all devoted to oral interchange of views, convictions, and confidences between representatives of the Democracy and friends of Mr. Hayes. There was no written agreement. Mr. Burke drew a MEMORANDUM, or the minutes of a *pour parler*, as they say in diplomacy, formulating the Southern understanding of the propositions and pledges as to the Southern policy which the friends of Mr. Hayes had orally advanced. This memorandum was read at a conference at Wormley's, * * * was then and there read, with the inquiry, '*Is this what you mean?*' and with the reply from Hayes' friends, '*Yes, substantially.*' Garfield is said to have made a *supplementary memorandum*, embodying certain dissents of his own from the *form of the document*, but not from its VITAL SUBSTANCE. But the main point is that this much exploited 'document' was nothing more than a *memorandum reciting the Southern understanding of the scope and purport of assurances made verbally by Foster and other friends of Hayes*, which assurances may be summarized in an expression written by Mr. Hayes himself to one of those friends, to wit: that, if inaugurated President, he would not employ the forces of the United States, physical or moral, to sustain or prop up any State government which was not sustained or acquiesced in by the mass of the people of the State itself, or words to that effect.

"There was no bargain. The Southern men accepted the honor of Charles Foster and Stanley Matthews as a guarantee for the good faith of Hayes *without collateral security of any kind*, and on the strength of that guarantee they resisted the policy of filibustering, allowed the count to proceed, accepted the decision of the Electoral Commission, and acquiesced in the inauguration of the President who was counted in. * * * Foster and Matthews were held sponsors for Hayes, and nobody else was regarded by the Southern men as speaking for him with either sincerity or authority. The letter of Hayes to Foster was the sole link that connected the former personally with the transaction. It was the basis of the understanding. It was the text of political scripture from which Matthews and Foster preached their glowing sermons of peace and good will. Undoubtedly they both went wide of its verbiage and long of its spirit in their own explications of the letter and their translations of Hayes' views, but they made *no promises which Mr. Hayes has not made history of*. It is not necessary to reproduce the text of either the letter or its explanatory memorandum. The conditions of both have been fulfilled, and the public can read them in the events which marked the first three months of the administration of Mr. Hayes. A. C. B."

The Washington *Union* of February 4 (Administration organ) corroborates Mr. Buell, saying: "We do not doubt for our own part that it is substantially a correct version of what took place."

WM. M. LEVY'S SPEECH.

Mr. Wm. M. Levy's speech, in House of Representatives, on Vermont vote, March 1, 1877.—(Record, page 2047.)

"The people of Louisiana have solemn, earnest, and, I believe, truthful assurances from prominent members of the Republican party, high in the confidence of Mr. Hayes, that, in the event of his election to the Presidency, he will be guided by a policy of conciliation toward the Southern States; that he will not use the Federal authority, or the army, to force upon those States governments not of their choice; but, in the case of these States, will leave their own people to settle the matter peaceably, of themselves. This, too, is the opinion of President Grant, which he freely expresses, and which, I am satisfied, he will carry out and adhere to. Under these circumstances, pretermitting, at least at this time, any discussion of the manner and means by which Mr. Hayes may secure the Presidency, satisfied from the action of Congress that his accession to the office is wellnigh an accomplished fact, I do not hesitate, for the reasons before stated, to declare that, actuated by a sense of duty to Louisiana, I shall throw no obstacle, by any action or vote of mine, in the way of the completion of the electoral count; but, relying upon the good faith, the integrity, and the truthfulness of the gentlemen who have given these assurances, and having faith in their individual personal honor, I shall unhesitatingly discharge this duty, and call upon those of my fellow-members who have been influenced in their action on this question by a desire to protect Louisiana and South Carolina, to join me in the course which I feel called upon and justified in pursuing."

A BLUNDER AT COLUMBUS.

[*New York Tribune, February* 24, 1877.]

WASHINGTON, *February* 23.—A copy of the *Ohio State Journal* of yesterday, published at Columbus, and received here to-day, contained an
editorial leader on the Louisiana question, in which a decided military
policy was advocated. It asserted that the State of Louisiana has been in
a condition of rebellion ever since the 14th of September, 1874, and urged
the President to recognize Governor Packard immediately, and sustain
him by the use of troops.

This article, published as it was at Governor Hayes' home, and in a
journal which is supposed to reflect in some degree his opinions, was circulated among the Democrats this afternoon, and caused great excitement
and alarm. Many of the more conservative men, who had been strength-
ened in the policy they have adopted by assurances they had received from
Governor Hayes' friends, were greatly shaken in their confidence in the
President elect. They were almost ready to join hands with the filibusters
unless they were assured that Governor Hayes was in no way responsible
for the sentiments above referred to. In order to ascertain the facts, Stanley Matthews, Charles Foster, and ex-Governor Dennison, of Ohio, sent
the following dispatch this afternoon, and received the answer that is ap-
pended:

"WASHINGTON CITY, *Feb'y* 23, 1877.

"JAMES M. COMLY,
   "*Columbus, Ohio:*

"The *Ohio State Journal* of yesterday was industriously circulated here
this morning among the Democratic members of the House, and soon after
a motion was made to take a recess until to-morrow, supported by an
almost solid Democratic vote, and carried. A caucus was called immediately. The article on Louisiana is supposed by them to have been inspired
by Governor Hayes, and to reflect his policy.
                              "STANLEY MATTHEWS,
                              "CHARLES FOSTER,
                              "WM. DENNISON."

———

"COLUMBUS, OHIO, *Feb'y* 23, 1877.

"The Hon. WM. DENNISON,
"STANLEY MATTHEWS, and
"CHAS. FOSTER.

"General Comly has been very sick for a week past. He is not per-
mitted to see or talk to any one, and your dispatch cannot be shown to
him. He is not allowed even to read anything that appears in the *State Journal.* The article in the *Journal* of Thursday, on Louisiana affairs, was
not written by him. Governor Hayes neither inspired it nor saw it, and
did not hear of it until his attention was called to it by your dispatch from
Washington.
                              "A. W. FRANCISCO,
                           "*Asso. Proprietor State Journal.*"

———

A dispatch was also received from General C. H. Grosvenor, speaker of
the Ohio house of representatives, saying that the article in question "was
originally a communication lying in the office, and was used by the
young men in charge of the office in the absence of General Comly, occasioned by severe illness."

———

"*Certainly no thought of influencing his action by furnishing these letters
ever occurred to me.*"—CHAS. FOSTER.

DEMOCRATIC PROOF THAT "THEY TRADED."

The New York *World* of March 26, 1877, says editorially:

"This exposure makes clear that Mr. Hayes, having virtually pledged himself in his letter of acceptance to make no political bargains for the Presidency, virtually pledged himself to a *political bargain* with his political opponents for the Presidency, and that he has failed, still fails, and will fail to carry that bargain out."

"The pledges were accepted; Senator Gordon accepted them for his own part, and Mr. Levy accepted them in a speech upon the floor of the House. They had their effect of *securing the peaceable completion of the count and the declaration of Hayes' election*."

"We are quite willing to believe that when Mr. Hayes assented to *this bargain* he fully meant to keep it."

"It appears that Senator Gordon, during the progress of the Electoral count in the House, called on Foster and said to him, that while he felt no responsibility for the action of the House, yet he should insist upon it that the South should have guarantees that their State governments should not be interfered with. They had contended for the past ten years for this right, and *if such pledges were not given* he would go into the House and urge upon his Southern friends to *assist in preventing the further count*. Gordon repeated that he was not responsible for what the House did, but he would *certainly favor filibustering* if there were not *guarantees* that the bayonet rule of the past eight years should be abolished. Mr. Foster replied that *all the necessary pledges would be given*."

"CERTAINLY NO THOUGHT OF INFLUENCING HIS ACTION BY FURNISHING THESE LETTERS EVER OCCURRED TO ME."—*Chas. Foster*.

———

The New York *World* of March 28, 1877, says editorially: "Mr. Matthews * * * made the pledge, and upon it certain Southern Democrats acted."

The New York *World* of March 29 says editorially: "Vicious, in the sense of public morals, as such a *bargain* and *trade* may have been, no one now doubts that by it Mr. Hayes became President, and that by it Mr. Evarts now acts as Secretary of State."

The New York *World* of March 27, 1877, says editorially: "The revelations made in regard to the *bargain* by which Mr. Hayes *purchased* the support of certain Southern Democrats during the progress of the Electoral count have created great excitement. * * * It seems clear, moreover, that other leading Republicans, notably Secretary Sherman and Congressman Garfield, are involved in this *bargain* to secure the acquiescence of the South in Mr. Hayes' inauguration. * * * The evidence on this point is said to be conclusive; and if it sustains the charge, the result of the revelation must be the *moral and political ruin* of the Republicans engaged in the *compact*. The treachery of such a *bargain* toward their allies disgraces them as partisans. The treachery toward those with whom they made the *treaty*, in refusing to carry out their *agreement*, disgraces them as men."

———

"If there be a mortal man in this *World* that says they traded I believe that that man lies."—*J. A. Garfield*.

"I told Mr. Foster that I wanted no *bargain*, no *agreement*; that I scorned the thought of it; * * * that I desired a *written assurance* from him!"—*John Young Brown*.

E. JOHN ELLIS' STATEMENT OF THE PRELIMINARY BARGAIN.

Published in Baltimore Sun and New York World, about March 28, 1877.

On the evening of the 20th of February Mr. Lamar sent a page to Mr. Ellis requesting an interview. On meeting Mr. Ellis, Mr. Lamar said that, in his opinion, the speech delivered by the Hon. Charles Foster that day was intended to be understood as the utterances of Gov. Hayes himself. He further said Judge Stanley Matthews had said to Foster that his (Foster's) speech was not strong enough, and that he should have said that Gov. Hayes would have nothing to do with Packard. Foster replied that he did not like to take so much upon himself, to which Matthews replied: "Well, if I had spoken I would have said so much, because it is the truth." Mr. Lamar said that it was the first utterances that he had ever heard from one of Gov. Hayes' friends important and direct enough to command attention from Southern people.

He advised Mr. Ellis to see Judge Matthews at once and then proceed to Columbus, Ohio, and if possible see and obtain of Gov. Hayes assurances and guarantees of a liberal and just policy toward Louisiana and South Carolina in the event of his inauguration. Mr. Ellis replied that he did not like to act without conference with his colleagues, but Mr. Lamar insisted that he did not believe in divided responsibilities, and urged Mr. Ellis to the course he had suggested. At the request of Mr. Ellis he wrote out in the form of a letter the substance of what he (Lamar) had said.

Mr. Ellis says: "I telegraphed that evening to Gov. Nicholls, informing him that a communication to him of great importance had reached me, and negotiations were opening up which might require me to go to Columbus and see Gov. Hayes, but that I would not go unless he sanctioned and telegraphed me a letter of authorization.

"Twenty-six hours afterward I received a reply from Gov. Nicholls, which I regarded as unsatisfactory, and showing plainly that he did not appreciate the importance of the communication, and betraying a hesitancy to accredit me to Gov. Hayes, and I resolved not to go any further with the affair: but I showed Mr. Lamar's letter to Major Burke, and advised him to see Judge Matthews and have a conference, and then to proceed to Columbus and see Gov. Hayes, in accordance with Mr. Lamar's original idea. Major Burke did see Judge Matthews, and arranged an interview, and invited me to accompany him. On the evening of the 25th or 26th of February Major Burke and the Hon. Henry Watterson, whom I had invited to accompany us, and myself, repaired to Wormley's, and in Judge Matthew's room we met him, ex-Gov. Dennison, of Ohio, Senator (now Secretary) Sherman, Chief-Justice Cartter, of the supreme court of the District, and Representatives Foster and Garfield.

"After some informal conversation, Judge Matthews asked me for an expression of opinion as to the desires and wishes of the people of the two Southern States, and in reference thereto our position and determination with regard to the electoral count. I stated to him, and to the gentlemen present, at some length, our unalterable determination to secure at all hazards the governments of Nicholls and Hampton, our earnest desire for the restoration of the right of self-government, and our great fear that Mr. Hayes, if inaugurated President, would use the troops for the purpose of maintaining Packard and Chamberlain, and it was upon this idea that I and my colleagues in Congress, as well as many Democratic Representatives, were filibustering to prevent the consummation of the count.

"Judge Matthews then entered into a lengthy and exhaustive review of the Southern question. He declared that he was the intimate friend, personal and political, of Gov. Hayes; that he was intimately acquainted with his views of the Southern question; that Gov. Hayes believed that the time had gone by for the maintenance of State governments with troops; that he desired that the States of South Carolina and Louisiana should have peace, home rule, and honest and stable governments, based upon the consent of the people most interested in good government; that he was tired of the strife, misrule, and dishonest governments and government officials, who had plundered these States; that he desired also to obliterate the color line in politics, as only in that way could the rights of the colored race be perfectly protected.

"He referred them to the letter of acceptance of Gov. Hayes, and to the speech of Hon. Chas. Foster, of the 20th of February, and declared that Gov. Hayes, if inaugurated President, would pursue the policy he had indicated. Then an autograph letter was shown me from Gov. Hayes to Charles Foster, thanking the latter for his speech in the House of Representatives, and declaring that if inaugurated President he would carry out toward the South the policy of peace and home rule as he (Foster) understood it.

"I then told Mr. Matthews that his views and those he attributed to Gov. Hayes were most gratifying to us, but there appeared to me a good deal of practical difficulty in carrying out these views. I told him, for instance, with regard to Louisiana, that the people who had voted for Hayes had voted for Packard; that the supporters of Tilden were the supporters of Nicholls; that the returning board which had assumed to award the vote of Louisiana to Hayes had awarded also a majority to Packard, and that I did not see how Mr. Hayes could consistently sustain Nicholls under the circumstances. He replied very quickly, I can see very easily how Nicholls can be sustained. I do not assume to speak absolutely for Gov. Hayes, but my policy would be to obtain from Nicholls assurances that the peace would be maintained, no one prosecuted on account of political offences, life, liberty, and property guaranteed to all; then withdraw the troops. Your people would then pay taxes only to Nicholls, while his government would grow firmly in authority, and Packard would starve to death for lack of money to support his government; and that, should it become necessary for the President to recognize any government in the State, he would find only one government in the State—that of Nicholls—and that, without inquiring into its original title, he would accept the fact and recognize it."

These assurances, Mr. Ellis says, were confirmed by every man present except Chief-Justice Cartter, who had left in the meantime.

THE COALITION.

Mr. W. R. Roberts announces the coalition in the New Orleans *Times* of March 7, 1877, by telegram from Washington of March 6: "The Administration leader in the Senate is not yet indicated. It may be Stanley Matthews, who is to succeed Sherman. Should Hayes, by disregarding the pledges of his managers, fail to pacify Louisiana and South Carolina, his Administration will open with deplorable difficulties. His only safety is thought to be to cling to the *coalition*, which, having the safety of these States in view, forced the count of the electoral vote to issue before the 4th of March. Honor and safety urge him to fulfil the pledges made for him by his managers."